TIDES OF JUSTICE

TIDES

OF JUSTICE

THE SUPREME COURT AND THE
CONSTITUTION IN OUR TIME

by ROBERT A. LISTON

 DELACORTE PRESS

TO SHERRY

CONTENTS

When I was in college, a visiting professor taught a course in constitutional law in which I enrolled. He announced the first day of class that he didn't particularly care whether his students showed up for lectures as long as they were there for the tests.

Such an opportunity was not to be wasted, and I hardly ever attended class. Instead, I went to the library and read constitutional law. I read and I read, devouring the great, historical decisions of the Supreme Court since *Marbury v. Madison.* I enjoyed it immensely and found that reading law is good training for a foggy mind and wavering concentration—and quite exciting, for legal opinions scintillate with life and argument and courage and great decision. My fascination for constitutional law was born there, and I received an "A" in the course—one of my few.

I can imagine teachers exclaiming, "Heavens! He's telling all the kids to skip classes." Hardly, although a day spent reading constructively at a library is scarcely misspent. I'm merely trying to suggest that Supreme Court opinions can be fun to read as well as informative.

In researching this book, I again delved deeply into lawbooks and again found the experience enjoyable. I remarked about this to a friend, who said, "You must be a frustrated lawyer." My reply: "No, I wouldn't want to be a lawyer, but I love the law."

Perhaps it would be more accurate to speak of love for the Supreme Court, for in that body there is reflected much of what is important and dramatic in government. Nobody draws a gun and shoots. No maiden swoons in the arms of her beloved. In fact there is hardly any action at all in the Supreme Court. Television producers and fiction writers would find it all a huge bore.

Yet, the Supreme Court has an abundance of conflict, and conflict is the essence of drama. In the Supreme Court the conflict takes the form of a clash between ideas. The opposing viewpoints which reach the high court are not so simple as right and wrong. Rather the clash is between two rights. Two ideas—both of which strong men may have fought and died for and both of which men of intelligence and good will value highly—are at war, and one of them has to lose. The decision can affect the lives, property, freedom and future of people around the world.

The drama of the Supreme Court stems, too, from the men and women involved in it. There is the conflict between the litigants, to be sure, but there is also the clash of personalities and ideas among the Supreme Court Justices themselves. They are flesh-and-blood men with passions and prejudices, virtues and faults who feel deeply and argue persuasively as they try to be wiser than any mortal should ever need to be in deciding right from right.

What is so remarkable to me about the Supreme Court as drama is that it is so very low-key. The Court is imprisoned in formality, procedure, gentlemanliness, which make the passions and angers and bold ideas and strong personalities stand out the more.

This book is about some of those ideas in collision. Most books about the Supreme Court end with the school-segregation case in 1954. This is understandable, for that decision almost certainly started a new era which is still in progress. No one knows when it will end or how it will turn out.

Yet, the era is over a decade old. Some great issues have developed during that time which are likely to remain before the Court and the nation for many years. This book is an attempt to discuss some of these great issues of our time, to relate their backgrounds, to give them some perspective and to estimate how they may develop in the future.

As such, this book is not history, not even contemporary history, if there is such a thing. There is no attempt here to trace the development of the Supreme Court. There is no discussion of the great issues of earlier times, the traces of which still remain in litigation before the Court. By this I refer to the momentous judicial battles fought over the meaning of interstate commerce, the right of government to legislate for the public welfare and to control business, of states' rights versus federal power.

This book is about today. It is an attempt to give the reader some understanding of the meaning and importance of Supreme Court decisions being made today and in the days ahead.

The second purpose of the book is to impart to you some sense of the drama of the Supreme Court and to encourage you to follow its activities and to read some Court opinions. A good one to start with is *Brown v. Board of Education of Topeka*—the school-segregation decision. It is short, simple, highly readable. Teachers should make it required reading in high school. There are many other highly literary opinions.

One tip: In all opinions there are passages containing references to other Court opinions. These are there largely for the benefit of lawyers and other judges, who will make use of the opinion in a legal and judicial way. As a layman, you can skip these technical aspects and get on to the good part.

In most books written for students and laymen about the Court, the authors omit the legal references to the cases, or they put them in notes at the rear of the book. Perhaps the authors or the publishers feel there is something frightening about a legal reference. There isn't. *Brown v. Board of Education of Topeka* has the legal reference of 347 U.S. 483. All this says is that the opinion of the Court may be found on page 483 in the 347th volume of United States Reports. *Engel v. Vitale,* the first school-prayer decision, has the legal reference of 370 U.S. 421. Go to any large library. The U.S. Reports are lined up in a row on a shelf. Pick the 370th volume and turn to page 421 and start to read.

Because I hope you will read some of these decisions, I have included whenever possible the legal references in the text as an aid to finding the opinion. If you aren't interested in pursuing the subject, then skip the references.

Another point: No effort has been made here to "sugar-coat" judicial writing. There may be a few words in use by the Supreme Court Justices that are unfamiliar, but I think not very many. Their sentence structure may occasionally be so involved as to make an admirer of good writing wince. The logic may require a second or third rereading of a particular passage in order to follow it. But all of this is part of the fun of constitutional law.

I hope you'll try.

My deepest thanks go to the kindly staffs at the Norwalk and Westport, Connecticut, public libraries and to Harry Hefferan, a fine member of the legal profession in Norwalk, who put me in touch with that marvelous man, Christy Hetherington, librarian of the Fairfield County, Connecticut, Law Library. Without his help and facilities, this book could not have been written.

ROBERT A. LISTON

I. CATALYST FOR CHANGE

Save our Republic, Impeach Earl Warren—Message on a roadside sign forty miles north of Utica, New York

On Lincoln's birthday in 1963, Earl Warren, Chief Justice of the United States, journeyed to Atlanta, Georgia, to make a major address. Thirty-six hundred students and faculty of the Georgia Institute of Technology, the famous Georgia Tech, gathered in Alexander Memorial Coliseum to hear the Chief Justice speak his thoughts on world peace and the rule of law.

The number who heard him was conspicuously swelled by armed guards brought in to protect the Chief Justice. There was twenty-five city detectives and uniformed guards in the auditorium, plus an unknown number of federal agents, all watching to see that no harm came to the nation's principal judicial officer.

Present in the auditorium was Dr. Henry G. Stilling, who headed an organization called the Atlanta Committee to Impeach Earl Warren. The night before, Dr. Stilling had gone to court to try to stop police from removing more than twenty large billboards his committee had erected in the Atlanta area. These signs, red, white and blue in color, read: HELP IMPEACH EARL WARREN. Dr. Stilling did not get his court order, but police said they did not intend to remove any signs erected on private property.

Such discourtesy to the nation's highest-ranking judiciary official was not limited to Georgia or to the South that year. On October 30 about seventy-five pickets marched for two hours in front of the New York City Bar Association Building at 42 West 44th Street in New York while awaiting the arrival of Chief Justice Warren. As they marched, the pickets shouted "Impeach Earl Warren" and carried placards urging the same action. Pamphlets were handed out reading, "Regardless of where Warren's personal sympathies lie, he has had—and still has—long-continued, powerful and open pro-Communist support."

The pamphlets also maintained that "violation of his oath of office to uphold and support the Constitution of the United States by decisions which visibly punched huge, ragged holes in the Constitution, supply ample legal grounds for the impeachment of Warren."

As Chief Justice Warren left the building, after making a short speech and being installed as an honorary member of the New York bar, the pickets hurled placards and leaflets at him and shouted for his impeachment.

Four days later the Reverend Francis E. Fenton, pastor of the Blessed Sacrament Church, in Connecticut, delivered a sermon on the "anti-Christ," in which he urged his parishioners to sign a petition calling for the impeachment of Chief Justice Warren. He received 674 signatures.

Nine days later Representative Robert T. Ashmore of South Carolina authored a bill in the House of Representatives to inscribe the words "In God We Trust" above the bench of the Supreme Court. Explained Representative Ashmore, "The Supreme Court should be made painfully aware of the fact there is an Authority higher than that of the Supreme Court of the United States."

Two weeks later, on Thanksgiving, motorists driving state route 12-D, between Boonville and Lowville, New York, about forty miles north of Utica, were surprised to see a large sign bearing the image of the American flag and the words "SAVE OUR REPUBLIC, IMPEACH EARL WARREN."

These are but a few of the actions taken by Americans to express their disagreement and displeasure with Supreme Court decisions. Many people took pen in hand to write down their feelings, but few so profitably as Eddie Rose, a student at the University of California at Los Angeles. He entered an essay contest sponsored by the John

Birch Society on the topic "Grounds for the Impeachment of Warren" and on February 5, 1962, won first prize of $1,000.

Others voiced their criticism in statistical terms. Senator James O. Eastland of Mississippi, chairman of the powerful Senate Judiciary Committee, figured out that the Court had upheld "the positions advocated by the Communist Party" or its sympathizers in 46 of 70 decisions, a .657 average. He even gave a breakdown for individual Justices, declaring Justice Hugo L. Black had rendered 102 what he termed "pro-Communist" votes and not one anti-Communist or "con" vote. Justice Felix Frankfurter had a record, according to Senator Eastland, of 69 pro and 34 con votes; Justice William O. Douglas, 97 pro and 3 con; Justice Tom C. Clark, 21 pro and 61 con; Chief Justice Warren, 62 pro and 3 con; Justice John Marshall Harlan, 30 pro and 35 con; Justice William J. Brennan, 49 pro and 2 con; Justice Charles Evans Whittaker, 12 pro and 30 con; Justice Potter Stewart, 5 pro and 14 con.

Senator Eastland, when questioned by his colleagues, declined to specify what he considered "pro-Communist," but stated his view that "the Chief Justice of the United States, when there is a clear-cut decision between the Communist Party and the security of the country, decides for the Communists."

Senator Eastland was far from alone in his denunciation of the Court and its decisions. "They put Negroes in the schools and now they've driven God out of them," cried Representative George Grant of Alabama. Representative Glenn Cunningham of Nebraska mouthed the phrase "Obscenity, yes! Prayer, no!" thus mimicking the Cuban revolutionary cry "Cuba, *si!* Yankee, no!"

Former President Herbert Hoover demanded a Constitutional amendment to legalize school prayers to stop "disintegration of a sacred American heritage." Senator Robert C. Byrd of West Virginia opined, "Somebody is tampering with America's soul. I leave it to you who that is."

The Reverend Billy Graham, the highly respected evangelist, said, following the Court decision to ban prayers in public schools: ". . . we will have to take the chaplains out of the armed forces, prayers cannot be said in Congress, and the President cannot put his hand on the Bible when he takes the oath of office."

Francis Cardinal Spellman of New York said he was "shocked and frightened" by the school-prayer decision and declared that it "strikes at the very heart of the Godly tradition in which America's children have for so long been raised."

Businessmen joined the storm of Court criticism. The general counsel for a large corporation said, "It pays to be a Negro or Communist if you want justice from the Warren Court. Businessmen don't get it."

The legal profession erupted with denunciation of the Court. A president of the American Bar Association lashed the Court for undermining "property rights," "internal security" and "good citizenship." The Conference of State Chief Justices formally voted to criticize the Court for its actions undermining the law in this country.

University law journals printed thousands of articles taking issue with points of law raised in Supreme Court opinions. Alan F. Westin, associate professor of law at Columbia University, writing in the New York *Times* in October 1962, reported that in the previous six months he had counted hostile editorials in 150 newspapers. He said twenty-five senators and seventy-five representatives had delivered attacks on the Court in Congress during that time.

Seldom before has the nation's high court been subjected to such a barrage of criticism and analysis. The Dred Scott decision of 1857, in which the Court held that Congress had no Constitutional power to forbid slavery in the new territories of the West, was so denounced by the public that the Court was eclipsed for decades. In the early 1930s the nine Supreme Court Justices gave such a narrow interpretation of the Constitution in voiding key pieces of New Deal legislation that President Franklin Delano Roosevelt tried to "pack" the court with as many as six extra judges. Roosevelt's plan kicked off a furor of reaction, mostly negative, and his plan was defeated.

Whether or not the current discussion about the Court is the most heated in its long history can be argued by historians. Certain it is that since May 17, 1954, when the Justices unanimously held school segregation to be unconstitutional, the nine men in their "marble palace" in Washington have lived in the eye of a public-opinion hurricane.

Each time the controversy seemed about to die from sheer public weariness with it a new decision fanned fresh discontent. After the order to desegregate schools came decisions pertaining to discrimination against Negroes in public life, outlining procedures in the arrest and conviction of persons accused of crime, protecting individuals who take the Fifth Amendment to avoid self-incrimination. Prayers and Bible reading were banned in public schools, and Congress and state legislatures were ordered to reapportion themselves.

These matters are the momentous constitutional issues of our time. They are history being made, not in one earth-shaking Supreme Court edict but in a series of individual decisions shaking judicial foundations and forming new legal ground. These judicial tremors are remaking whole segments of our society, our institutions and our attitudes—and doing it now, this very minute, as you read.

School desegregation, the oldest of the major issues to be discussed in this book, has been called the single most important decision ever made by an American court—or any court, for that matter. It made illegal existing educational policy in all the former Confederate states and in much of the North and West. Formerly segregated schools had to be integrated, sometimes with the force of federal arms, as in Little Rock, Arkansas, and Oxford, Mississippi. The decision gave hope to Negroes that their "second-class" citizenship could end and sparked the Negro revolution in America with its boycotts, sit-ins, lie-ins, and other forms of civil disobedience, demonstrations of wide variety and judicial and legislative battles.

Volumes could be written on the aftermath of May 17, 1954, and doubtlessly will be. These books will most certainly want to mention that one of the more long-lasting, if subtler, effects of the decision was to cause millions of white Americans to become aware of the injustice being done to Negro citizens and to start the difficult tasks of correction and adjustment. Much of what has occurred since 1954 has been part of the larger process whereby the races, historically and culturally separated in this country, are learning to live together in equality.

If school desegregation was immoral and illegal, what of racial discrimination in all its forms? May the proprietor of a privately owned restaurant catering to the public refuse to serve Negroes? May a store which sells to Negroes in all its departments refuse to serve them at its lunch counter? Can a hotel or motel refuse to

provide accommodations for a Negro family? A theater to sell seats?
A barber to cut hair?

Questions broaden in scope. Must an employer hire a certain
percentage of Negroes? Must a landlord rent his homes to at least
some Negroes? Must a church take in Negro members? How about a
fraternal organization?

Like ripples on a glassy pond, the questions proliferate—and most
are far from settled, either legally or morally. These will be the court
battles of the years ahead, as the nation wrestles with its conscience
and seeks to equate private opinion with public necessity. The result
can only be continued changes in our patterns of employment,
housing, entertainment and social relations—in all of which the
courts will be deeply involved.

When the Supreme Court, in 1962 and 1963, prohibited prayers
and Bible reading in public schools, it opened a Pandora's box of
troubles, in addition to creating perhaps the greatest public clamor
in its history. Under fire are all sorts of public prayers, mottoes on
coins and public buildings, the wording of the Pledge of Allegiance,
use of chaplains in the military service and a host of other religious
manifestatons in our everyday life. Court cases have already been
brought aimed at removing tax exemptions for churches and to end
other forms of public subsidies to church-owned colleges, hospitals
and other institutions. Such court suits, if won, could greatly change
certain public forms of religious worship in this country, as well as
affect conventional attitudes toward religion and morality.

Court decisions affecting criminal procedures have, in the opinion
of police and prosecutors, brought sharp increases in crime rates—
15 per cent over a two-year period. A man accused of crime now has
improved safeguards against illegal searches and seizures, confessions being pressured out of him and being used against him at his
trial, denial of his right to see a lawyer and improper use of
evidence by prosecutors—and many other procedures. Capturing
and convicting criminals is now much more difficult.

The result—besides controversy—has been to force changes in
trial procedures and police methods so as to protect individual
rights. Another result has been the release of obviously guilty men
on what seems to the public to be "technicalities," giving rise to this
question: Exactly how far must police and criminal courts go to

defend the individual at the expense of society's need to have laws obeyed? This question will be a long, long time in the answering.

Closely related is the question of man's rights under the Fifth Amendment. The Supreme Court has, in sweeping—and widely denounced—decisions, sharply limited the power of legislative committees to force a witness to talk when he wishes to remain silent. That right to silence is his under the Bill of Rights—a right being used by professional racketeers and subversives to escape justice. Again, must society submerge its right to know and its need to protect itself from those who would pervert or destroy it in order to protect individuals taking advantage of constitutional rights? Argument over the answer will continue for years, creating many, many court cases.

Some observers believe the Court's 1962, 1963 and 1964 rulings on reapportionment of Congress and state legislatures may cause changes in America greater even than school desegregation. The rulings were the death knell for rural control of legislatures. The decisions mean at the very least that the voices of the city and suburbs will become dominant in legislatures. Greater effort to resolve gnawing urban problems—such as poverty, poor housing, inferior sanitation, disease, inadequate educational and recreational facilities—cannot help but be made.

In a larger realm, the reapportionment rulings of the Supreme Court will doubtless bring pronounced political shifts. Rural politicians, who for decades have controlled state legislatures and, sometimes, even Congress, will no longer be able to do so. Machine politicians should have a more difficult time "delivering the vote." Thus, the type of campaigning and the quality of candidates running for office should change. Finally, some observers predict that once state legislatures become more sensitive to public opinion, the country will undergo a return to states' rights and a lessening of federal domination.

It would be an exaggeration to say that the Supreme Court is leading the nation into a critical re-examination of our national attitudes and institutions, including some previously thought inviolate. Such re-examination is taking place all right and the Court has an important role in it. But it is more likely that the Court is merely correctly judging the temper of the times. The "grass roots" desire for national self-analysis and improvement swept John F. Kennedy into office and continues the dominant influence in the White House, Congress, many gubernatorial mansions and in city halls across the land. The result is an exciting, dynamic time in which to live and participate.

History, at least the portion of it the Supreme Court is writing, has seldom had such a colorful cast of characters. There is Madalyn Murray, a woman who seemed to be hungering for revenge and notoriety and finding it all—and much more she did not bargain for—in the school-prayer cases.

There is Danny Escobedo, a scared twenty-two-year-old Chicagoan of Mexican extraction, accused of murdering his sister's husband. Danny would ordinarily be an individual of minuscule importance, except that he asked to see his lawyer as police were questioning him and was refused.

Clarence Earl Gideon, a lifelong failure, a human derelict on the sea of life, found his way into history because he comprehended a constitutional principle of immense importance: No man should be tried without a lawyer.

Dollree Mapp, a Cleveland, Ohio, mother, entered history books kicking and scratching police who sought to arrest her. She snatched a "warrant" out of a policeman's hand and shoved it down into the bosom of her dress, which provoked police action that makes fascinating reading even in a Supreme Court decision.

Then there is Thurgood Marshall, calm, relaxed, "cool," "loose," informal of speech, dedicated to puncturing the balloons of pretentiousness. As attorney for the National Association for the Advancement of Colored People, this immense individual stalks through history. He believed segregation and discrimination were unconstitutional and he worked and schemed, plotted and prepared for years to win his point—and freedom for his people.

This "cast of characters" worked in settings that is the stuff of fiction. Imagine a poorly executed theft of coins from a jukebox and a Coke machine, as well as "a small amount of beer and some wine," from a sleazy pool room in Panama City, Florida, producing a constitutional question that would lead to the Marble Palace of the Supreme Court. Or imagine a group of college kids advancing the cause of human liberty by trying to ride a merry-go-round in an amusement park.

Yet, all the people and problems that go before the Supreme Court pale before the natural drama of the men who sit there. Consider the man himself, Chief Justice Earl Warren, so trusted for his fair-mindedness that California voters twice nominated him for Governor on both the Democratic and Republican tickets. This man, having lived threescore years and ten, most of it devoted to serving his fellow citizens and the law, has been denounced in terms that would not be used against a criminal.

Consider Tom C. Clark, whose appointment as Associate Justice by President Truman was widely denounced as unworthy. Yet he has become a great figure in American law, particularly devoted to upgrading the standards of the courts and law enforcement all over the country. There is Justice John Marshall Harlan, grandson of a Supreme Court Justice. The grandfather wrote a series of memorable dissents. The grandson is writing a series of memorable dissents.

There is Justice William O. Douglas, outdoorsman, naturalist, author of twenty best-selling books and a conspicuous advocate of libertarian views. In over a quarter century on the high court he has left an indelible mark in defense of individual and economic liberty.

There is Justice Hugo Lafayette Black, a man almost a legend in his own time. Born into humble surroundings in Alabama, he came to the Court after serving as a prosecuting attorney and United States Senator. His appointment by President Franklin D. Roosevelt was far from popular, with business and conservative groups denouncing the New Deal Senator. Then a charge was made that he was a racist because he had once held membership in the Ku Klux Klan. Justice Black explained that he had joined many organizations while running for political office, that he had never attended a Klan meeting and had no sympathy with the organization. The KKK membership is still brought up after thirty years by those who hope, somehow, to impugn his reputation.

Damaging the reputation of Mr. Justice Black takes some doing, for in nearly threescore years on the Court, at the age of seventy-nine, he is, more than any other man, the architect of the Court's tower of justice. In the 1930s and 1940s and 1950s, he and Justice

Douglas wrote powerful dissents in which they held firm for individual liberty and human rights they felt were inalienable. Now those dissents are being written into law. On issue after issue, Justice Black and Justice Douglas are seeing their views adopted by the majority of the Court and public opinion of the nation.

A man of seemingly boundless energy—he is a famous tennis player—Justice Black has been a peppery judicial figure, surrounded much of his life by the controversy that has swirled about the Court in its moments of great decisions. His recent moves away from civil libertarian positions, most notably in the case on park segregation, continue his controversial reputation.

In the autumn of 1966 the other Justices of the Court included John M. Harlan, Byron R. White, William J. Brennan, Jr., Potter Stewart and Abe Fortas. It is relatively sure that the more recently appointed Justices will carry on those attitudes of clarity and force which have characterized the Court in recent years.

Much of the abuse heaped on the Court is political grandstanding, intemperateness, error and misunderstanding by those who dislike a particular decision. Some criticism, seen largely in law journals, is correct and well thought out, but it is hindsight, "Monday-morning quarterbacking" and important only as legal gymnastics. In this category is the dreary drizzle of comments that the Justices would have been wiser to use article so and so or amendment such and such of the Constitution instead of the one they chose in deciding the case.

Deserving of far more consideration are those criticisms which deal with the role of the Supreme Court in our national life. More specifically, is the Court acting as a nine-man super-legislature enacting its own opinions into law? Is the Court usurping the powers of Congress, thus creating major changes in our form of government?

There are other questions being raised about the role of the court, questions which underlie all the momentous judicial issues of our times. These underlying questions are the subject of the next chapter.

II. THE LIMITS OF POWER

> *No Supreme Court in American history has ever defied for long the sustained will of dominant opinion in the nation.*—Professor Alan F. Westin of Columbia University

Law, as practiced in this country and England, is a game in which everything that has gone before counts. Taking a case to court is like going into the seventh game of the World Series with two outs in the ninth inning. You are expected to know not only the score, what happened in that and previous innings and in preceding games of the series, but also the events of every game that has ever been played, not just by your club but by every major and minor, professional and amateur team that ever took a field anywhere in the Unites States.

The law is much like that. Naturally, every lawyer doesn't know all this information, but it is all recorded for him in law libraries. To prepare for a case, the proper lawyer goes to the library—or pays someone else to do it for him—to "read law"—that is, find out what has happened in the law games preceding his. What are the various ways a man has been called out at second base? How many balks have been called with two out and the bases loaded in the top of the third inning?

If a lawyer is pleading a simple divorce case, he must know all the rules governing divorce and the results of all the preceding divorce trials that were even remotely similar to the case he is bringing into court. If he is filing suit for damages resulting from an automobile accident, he must know all the laws governing such litigations and the results of preceding cases similar to his. If he is seeking to have school segregation declared illegal, he must know the results of every such case ever filed—or at least those that tend to support his position. The opposing lawyers, if they are good, will concentrate on the results which aid their viewpoint.

If you get the impression that a computer would make a good lawyer, you are right—up to a point. Many a lawyer has wished for a computer so programmed as to give him in a second all results of pertinent cases. Think of the time he would save.

The word for all this is *precedent*, or, as the lawyers say, *stare decisis*, which means "to abide by former cases." That which has gone before is binding in each succeeding trial. Continuity of the law is an absolute necessity, or we would all be at the whim of a judge and jury. When you are arrested for speeding you count on the fact that the judge will require the motorcycle policeman to swear that he clocked you at fifty miles an hour in a thirty-five-mile zone or that he used radar or some other legally acceptable means to establish how fast you were going. You count on the fact that the judge will not suddenly declare that a fortuneteller using a crystal ball is evidence of your guilt. If the judge tried to do so, you would stand up and scream, "Objection! There is no precedent for that." And you would be right.

If you wish to have school segregation declared illegal and the precedents are all against you, what do you do then? Is there no way to change the past? Yes. One way is for the legislature or Congress to pass legislation changing the law. But this has not been done; besides, you believe it is not the law that is wrong but the court's interpretation of it. You say in effect: "Some judge made a mistake in the beginning and it has been compounded ever since. It is time to correct all these mistakes by declaring school segregation illegal."

Doing this would be like declaring speedometers and radar gauges illegal and specifying the use of crystal balls to find speeders. Everything would be turned topsy-turvy. Police methods would have to be changed. Your speedometer would be of no value. Industry would have to be geared to turn out crystal balls, and high schools would need to offer night courses in crystal-ball soothsaying.

To upset a century of saying that school segregation is legal is much the same. Schools, classrooms, teachers, books, athletic schedules, nearly everything involved in a modern educational system would have to be revised. Public attitudes would have to be changed drastically. The expense and turmoil would be great indeed.

If you wish to change the interpretation of the law to make school segregation illegal, you must have an extremely good reason to do so. You must find some precedents, some history to justify this expense and turmoil, or some overpowering legal logic to justify all this trouble.

The important word is *legal*. A legal reason is different from one nonlawyers would think of. You might argue that school segregation is immoral, unethical, unlikely to result in good education, psychologically damaging to both white and Negro children, and wasteful of tax money.

If you went before the Supreme Court with such arguments, the Justices might privately agree with you, but they would interrupt before you had hardly started to ask for a legal reason.

You must provide a legal argument based upon the law and the Constitution. Such an argument might be that school segregation deprives Negro children of equal protection under the law as guaranteed in the 14th Amendment to the Constitution. If you argued convincingly enough, you might even convince a nine-judge panel of the Supreme Court. If you wish to have prayers and Bible recitations banned from public schools, you might argue that this violates the First Amendment's prohibition against the establishment of religion and, if you are convincing enough, you might persuade the Supreme Court of the United States.

Perhaps the soundest argument against the Warren Court—whether or not that argument is correct—is that the legal reasons used to overturn long-standing Court rulings have been insufficient and unconvincing.

Another strong argument against the Warren Court is that it has seriously undermined our federal system of government.

As you know, the United States is a federation of fifty states which have surrendered a portion of their sovereignty to a central, or federal, government. The federal government represents all the states collectively in foreign relations, military affairs, interstate commerce, currency and other matters spelled out in the Constitution.

Since the states united to form the federal government there has been a gradual usurpation of power by the federal government at the expense of state power—or, as it is usually called, "states' rights."

This growth of federal power has been accomplished with the approval of and, often, the encouragement of the Supreme Court, which has been asked to pass upon the constitutionality of many legislative acts extending federal power. These Supreme Court decisions were nearly all bitterly contested and frequently denounced.

They broadened the meaning of interstate commerce, and applied the guarantees of the Bill of Rights and the Fourteenth Amendment to the states, widened the meaning of the due process or equal-protection clauses of the Fifth and Fourteenth Amendments. The increase in federal power at the expense of states' rights has been going on since shortly after the turn of the century. It was greatly accelerated in the administrations of Franklin D. Roosevelt, and there has been no notable slowdown since.

The contention that the Warren Court has increased federal power at the expense of state authority is not very new or terribly surprising. The arguments heard over the past thirty years concerning preservation of states' rights are beginning to be wearying. These are that the President and Congress, with the blessing of the Supreme Court, have altered the federal form of government intended by our forefathers who framed the Constitution. The result is a less democratic government, centered in a behemoth federal bureaucracy which is less easily controlled by voters than individual state governments. This government is, the argument goes, power hungry, wasteful and stultifying.

In the nearly thirty-five years that this argument has gone on, all but the most recalcitrant states'-righters have had to admit that voters have shown, in repeated elections of both Democrats and Republicans, that they like the changes that have been made, that they visualize the United States as one nation rather than as a federation of individual states, and that they believe the federal, rather than the state, level is the proper place to resolve many of our economic and social problems.

When a Southern congressman denounces school desegregation as interfering with states' rights he is rephrasing a vintage and largely discredited argument. A much more inspired and serious charge is that the Warren Court has not only reduced state sovereignty but has also tried to remake the states in the federal image. Not only has the high court outlawed segregation in schools, according to this argument, but it has also tried to specify the ways and means by which schools shall be desegregated. Not only has the Supreme Court declared that state legislatures shall be reapportioned, but it has also set itself up as judge of that reapportionment and in some instances specified how the reapportionment shall be done.

There are critics who, while not overly affected by the traditional loss of states' rights, are concerned about the growth of federal judicial power. They are particularly concerned that the Warren Court has "federalized" the state courts.

The United States has a dual court system. We are governed by two sets of laws—state and federal. Mostly we are governed by state laws. Exceed the speed limit, fail to maintain proper sanitary conditions in your home, "hook" school, fail to get a proper marriage license or get sued for damages because you threw rocks at your neighbor's greenhouse—all these and hundreds more are state-court matters.

You will be haled into federal court when you violate federal laws, by failing to pay income taxes, striking in violation of the Taft-Hartley law, violating federal wage and hour laws, burning a draft card, infringing on an indiivdual's civil rights, committing a crime in interstate commerce, leaving the state as a fugitive and other matters.

The situation becomes more complex because federal and state laws overlap. For example, suppose a city fireman entered your home to inspect for fire hazards, then suddenly whipped out a badge, declared himself an auxiliary policeman and arrested you for operating a "still" in the kitchen. Hauled into state courts, you could quite properly maintain that the search and seizure violated your rights under the Fourth Amendment to the Constitution, which reads: "The right of the people to be secure in their persons, houses, paper and effects, against unreasonable searches and seizures, shall not be violated, and no warrants shall be issued but upon probable cause, supported by oath or affirmation, and particularly describing the place to be searched, and the person or things to be seized." The state judge hearing your case would be required to rule on the federal question you had raised, and his opinion could be appealed in the federal courts, perhaps all the way to the Supreme Court.

One of the criticisms made of the Warren Court is that it has, in its far-reaching decisions relative to self-incrimination and criminal procedure, severely tampered with the state courts. Many critics have attacked the Court for forcing the federal model on the state courts.

The fifty state court systems have developed in different ways. They have varying laws and peculiar procedures, developed in accordance with individual state traditions and needs. In decision after decision, as will be itemized in succeeding chapters, the high court has, according to critics, altered these state procedures to make them like the federal courts. Hundreds of law professors have written articles decrying this tendency.

One of the more persistent and serious arguments raised against the Supreme Court in recent years is that it has usurped the legislative prerogatives of Congress and is writing new laws. This is an old argument, raised by anyone who dislikes a particular high-court decision. But the argument has never been raised so frequently as in recent years.

For example, if the people of the United States had wanted to see school segregation abolished, they would have called on Congress to do so. Or, stated another way: If Congress had wanted to have school segregation abolished, it could easily have done so by enacting a law to that effect. Congress did not do so; therefore nine Justices of the Supreme Court had no right to distort the meaning of the Constitution to enact their own opinions into law.

If Congress had wanted to insist that its members be elected from districts approximately equal in population, it could have done so. The Justices had no constitutional right to bypass Congress and order redistricting to take place. The same logic is applied to court decisions on school prayers, discrimination, and criminal procedures.

The critics maintain that the Supreme Court, composed of nine men, is legislating upon these sensitive matters, rather than Congress. This, it is contended, is undemocratic and violates the intent of the Constitution. Precedents dangerous for our democratic institutions, in particular for the Supreme Court, are being set.

All that you have read in this chapter about legal precedents, our dual governmental system, and judicial "legislation" are but three legs of the central court issue of our times: judicial restraint versus judicial activism. Simply stated, the advocates of judicial restraint say the Court should go slowly in upsetting judicial precedents, in altering federal-state relationships and in imposing the judges' wills upon Congress and the state legislatures. The judicial activists see the high court as an arm of government equal with the Presidency and Congress and quite entitled to use its considerable powers to shape our institutions in accordance with the will of the people and the framers of the Constitution.

Principal advocate of judicial restraint was the late Felix Frankfurter, for twenty years an Associate Justice and one of the great figures in American law. His retirement in 1962 and death in 1965 ended an era of the Supreme Court, during which time his views in favor of judicial restraint were often controlling and always meaningful.

"Judicial power," said Justice Frankfurter in a 1958 dissenting opinion, ". . . must be on guard against encroaching beyond its proper bounds, and not the less so since the only restraint upon it is self-restraint. When the power of Congress to pass a statute is challenged, the function of this Court is to determine whether legislative action lies clearly outside the constitutional grant of power. . . . It is not the business of this Court to pronounce policy. It must observe a fastidious regard for limitations on its own power and this precludes the Court's giving effect to its own notions of what is wise or politic. Self-restraint is of the essence in the observance of the judicial oath, for the Constitution has not authorized the judges to sit in judgment on the wisdom of what Congress and the Executive Branch do."

Another time Justice Frankfurter wrote of his intention to "use this opinion as a vehicle for preaching the true democratic faith of not relying on the Court for the impossible task of assuring a vigorous, mature, self-protecting and tolerant democracy by bringing the responsibility for a combination of firmness and toleration directly home where it belongs—to the people and their representatives themselves."

As you read on in this book—and hopefully Supreme Court opinions themselves—you will find these views of judicial restraint expressed repeatedly by Justice Frankfurter and by Justice Harlan, generally viewed as his successor as advocate of judicial restraint.

No less concerned for the Constitution and our democracy are the political activists, in particular Justices Black and Douglas and Chief Justice Warren. The activists believe that the Court has a duty to act whenever a constitutional issue comes before it, a duty it cannot escape by modest deference to the view of other branches of government. More, they believe (at least some of the time) that the Court must fight injustice wherever it occurs. In succeeding chapters you will see this view expressed in terms of school segregation, equal representation and other matters. Thus, in *Bell v. Maryland,* Justice Douglas sharply attacked his colleagues for failing to answer a key legal question in regard to racial discrimination, saying that the Court's failure (restraint) weakens the "prestige of law in the life of the Nation."

The activists are most concerned about individual liberty. Justice Black defends certain individual liberties as "absolute." No court, no law, no other individual, no need of society, can limit freedom of speech, religion, etc. Said Justice Black, "The phrase 'Congress shall make no law' (as in the First Amendment) is composed of plain words, easily understood. The Framers knew this. . . . To my way of thinking, at least, the history and language of the Constitution and the Bill of Rights . . . make it plain that one of the primary purposes of the Constitution with its amendments was to withdraw from the Government all power to act in certain areas." In other words, no law, to Justice Black, means no law—none at all.

Down through history Justice Black's words will ring in the ears of every man who loves liberty and looks to the Bill of Rights and the Constitution to insure it. "Under our Constitutional system," he wrote in a 1939 opinion, long before Chief Justice Warren's term began, "courts stand against any winds that blow as havens of refuge for those who might otherwise suffer because they are helpless, weak, outnumbered, or because they are nonconforming victims of prejudice and public excitement. . . . No higher duty, no more solemn responsibility, rests upon this Court than that of translating into living law and maintaining this constitutional shield deliberately planned and inscribed for the benefit of every human being subject to our Constitution—of whatever race, creed or persuasion."

The pages of history, just as are the annals of the Supreme Court, must be enlivened by the battles waged over judicial restraint versus judicial activism. Much of what you read in succeeding chapters will be skirmishes over these two concepts. No particular foresight is required to predict that this battle will be waged during the rest of our lives.

It is not an academic battle, for the future of the Supreme Court will be determined by the manner in which the fray is waged. The Court, like the President and Congress, serves at the pleasure of the American people. "Their power is enormous," Alexis de Tocqueville wrote of the Justices of the Supreme Court over a century ago, "but it is the power of public opinion."

Indeed! The Supreme Court has no army to enforce its decisions. It is dependent on the executive branch to carry out its orders. If the President refuses—as Jefferson and Jackson did—or if states refuse, either directly or indirectly, the Justices have no way to force their will on the people or public officials.

In fact, frustrating the high court's wishes is a rather finely developed art in this country. Congress does it regularly. For instance, federal courts are burdened with negligence cases involving railroad and maritime workers. Such employees when injured on the job, have to prove the mishap was caused by their employers' negligence. The question of negligence is appealed to courts, often reaching the Supreme Court. All other types of workmen receive compensation without proving negligence. But Congress refuses to grant the same privilege to railroad and maritime workers, thus relieving the courts of these bothersome cases.

The U.S. Patent Office is peerless at frustrating the Supreme Court. Patents are issued regularly to an implausible array of gadgets and gimmicks which individuals have "invented." Many times the question of whether the gadget is an honest-to-goodness invention or only imitative of another reaches the Supreme Court.

With clocklike regularity the high court has invalidated patents such as those issued for a clay doorknob shaped slightly differently from other doorknobs, a collar made of parchment paper instead of linen, fine threads placed across the squares in a hairnet to keep the hair in place, a stamp for impressing initials on the side of a plug of tobacco, a revolving cue rack, rubber hand grips on bicycle handlebars, and an oval roll of toilet tissue.

In case after case the Justices have made their position clear that issuing patents to such imitative junk was an affront to the Constitution. Justice Douglas observed in one case, "The patent involved in the present case belongs to the list of incredible patents which the Patent Office has spawned. The fact that a patent as flimsy and as spurious as this one [a three-sided wooden frame used by supermarket cashiers to pull groceries toward the cash register] has to be brought all the way to this Court to be declared invalid, dramatically illustrates how far our patent system frequently departs from the Constitutional standards which are supposed to govern."

Does the acid comment of the high-court Justices deter the Patent Office from issuing ridiculous patents? It does not. The Court has no power to reach into the Patent Office—or any other agency of state and federal government—and cause them to reform their policies—except the power of public opinion.

What might be called bureaucratic disobedience is only one of the checkreins on the power of the Court. Its rulings can be altered by constitutional amendment. The Sixteenth Amendment legalizing the income tax is a direct result of a Supreme Court decision declaring the tax unconstitutional.

Congress has great power over the Court. It can enact legislation that reverses Court decisions. It can change the makeup of the Court by adding Justices, as President Franklin Roosevelt tried to have done in 1937. Or Congress can change the laws governing the types of cases which can be appealed to the Supreme Court. In recent years several attempts have been made to curb the Court's power in this way.

The chief curb on the Court is the President's power to appoint Justices and the Senate's right to approve the appointments. Every President has sought to appoint Justices whom he feels agree with his political, economic and social philosophies. Many times Presidents have been disappointed in their appointments. Their "liberal" Justice turned out to be a "conservative" one. But the appointment power remains the main way court opinions are changed. President Roosevelt changed the Court's attitude not by packing it but by appointing liberal-minded men to replace conservative Justices who retired or died.

The opinions of lawyers and judges have considerable effect on the Court. Bar journals published by leading law schools are read by Justices. The views of distinguished legal scholars cannot help but color the thinking of the men in their Marble Palace.

Thus, whenever you hear about the uncontrolled power of the Supreme Court, don't believe it. The Court has no power other than public opinion or, as Dr. Alan F. Westin, Professor of Government at Columbia University, New York, has stated, "No Supreme Court in American history has ever defied for long the sustained will of dominant opinion in the Nation."

Professor Westin goes on to define "dominant opinion" as the "active consensus of an era as represented in the 'passionate truths' held by the majority of elected and state officials, the leaders of the most influential economic, civic and religious groups, and those mass media (newspaper, magazines, etc.) trusted by the politically active public."

It is safe to say that no schools will be desegregated, no religious prayers eliminated from schools, no prisoners released because of improper searches, no legislatures reapportioned unless the *dominant opinion* wants this to take place. That these steps have been and are being taken is the best available evidence that the Supreme Court reflects that dominant opinion.

The fear is that the Court, if it pursues its judicial activism, will eventually overstep and collide with the will of the people. If this occurs, the Court will run the risk of legislative curtailment or other curbs.

In the years ahead, the Court's relationship to public opinion will be a matter to watch.

III. ATTACKING THE CITADEL
OF SEGREGATION

Our Constitution is color-blind, and neither knows nor tolerates classes among citizens.—Justice John Marshall Harlan, dissenting in PLESSY V. FERGUSON

When Thurgood Marshall walked into the national headquarters of the National Association for the Advancement of Colored People (NAACP) in 1938 and took over as special counsel, he thought of it as a "very tush-tush" place. Marshall later described what he meant by "tush-tush" in these words:

"You should have seen it, yeh, you should have seen it. It was Dr. Whosis and Mr. Whatsis and all kinds of nonsense like that, bowing and scraping like an embassy scene. You really should have been there. Well, I took a long look, not too long, but long enough, and I figured I'd have to bust that stuff up pretty quick. Believe me, I had 'em talking first names in nothin' time and no more of that formality business."

Marshall was thirty years old and a big man physically. He was six feet, two inches tall and weighed over two hundred pounds. He had a tremendous capacity for work—he later commented, "Isn't it nice that no one cares which twenty-three hours a day I work?"— and a phenomenal ability to enjoy life. He liked Western movies, detective stories, a blaring phonograph, good friends and companionship.

He was "at home" anywhere. One colleague said of him, "Thurgood is as comfortable at the Hogwash Junction function as he is in the home of a Supreme Court Justice. He relates to everybody and anybody and it's this, more than anything else, that sets him apart from other men."

He has been described as calm, cool, collected and casual, and he has said of himself, "I intend to wear life like a very loose garment and never worry about nothin'."

Those who looked for formality of language or dress or demeanor from the new special counsel of the NAACP in 1938 were due for a disappointment. But if they looked for a good lawyer, they were in for a most pleasant surprise, for, as one New York attorney has said of Marshall, "Behind all that garrulousness, chuckling, hooting and hollering, there lurks a powerful, incisive legal mind."

Thurgood Marshall was born in Baltimore, Maryland, in 1908, the great-grandson of a slave. Marshall has described this ancestor in terms that cannot be surpassed: "His more polite descendants like to think he came from the cultured tribes in Sierra Leone, but we all know he really came from the toughest part of the Congo."

Marshall's forebear was seized by a white big-game hunter and brought to the eastern shore of Maryland, where he was far from docile. Finally, as Thurgood Marshall describes it, the owner said, "Look, I brought you here, so I guess I can't very well shoot you—as you deserve. On the other hand, I can't with clear conscience sell anyone as vicious as you to another slaveholder. So I'm going to set you free—on one condition. Get out of this county and never come back. And that is the only time Massuh didn't get an argument from the old boy."

Marshall's mother was a schoolteacher and his father was a writer and part-time country-club steward. He was also a great influence in the young Thurgood's life. "My father made a lawyer of me," he says. "He did it by teaching me to argue, by challenging my logic on every point, by making me prove every statement. He never told me to become a lawyer, but he turned me into one."

After graduating from Douglass High School in Baltimore and graduating with honors from Lincoln University in Chester County,

Pennsylvania, where he worked his way through as a grocery clerk, dining-car waiter and baker, he entered Howard University in Washington, D.C., where "for the first time I found out my rights." He earned his law degree in 1933 and passed the Maryland state bar. That same year he entered private practice in Baltimore and quickly built up the largest practice in that city. But he received so little in legal fees that he couldn't pay his rent.

From the beginning his interests lay in the civil-rights field. As early as 1935 he brought a lawsuit which forced the University of Maryland Law School to admit a Negro student. In 1936 he became a field assistant to Charles Hamilton Houston, a Harvard Law School graduate and dean of the Howard University Law School who, as special counsel to the NAACP, was "the Moses" of the civil-rights movement. Houston recruited, trained and inspired most of the Negro attorneys who later fought the rights movement through the courts, including the man who was to replace him as special counsel, Thurgood Marshall.

In the depths of the Great Depression of the 1930s, the NAACP, under the legal leadership of Houston and then Marshall, set out to eliminate white supremacy in American life—by legal means. Theirs was a nearly hopeless task, requiring the best in legal talent and a great deal of money. To get the latter, the NAACP set up the Legal Defense and Education Fund, a unit technically divorced from the Association's propaganda and legislative activities. Marshall became general counsel to the Fund, which grew from modest beginnings until, in 1950, it had $150,000 a year to prosecute civil-rights cases throughout the country.

The talent came too. Negro legal minds such as William Hastie, later to become a Judge of the United States Court of Appeals; James Nabrit, who became Dean of Howard Law School; Ralph Bunche, the celebrated United Nations diplomat; William R. Ming, who became a famous professor of law at the University of Chicago and a reknowned attorney in that city; Spottswood Robinson III, a Richmond lawyer; Loren Miller of Los Angeles; George Vaughn of St. Louis; Oliver Hill in Virginia; and Jack Greenberg, who became Marshall's assistant. There were many others.

The NAACP assaulted segregation on several fronts. They attacked the system of "white primaries," restrictive covenants in housing, "Jim Crow" in transportation, as well as school segregation. Each of these different forms of racial segregation was an application of the "separate but equal" rule laid down in a celebrated Supreme Court decision *Plessy v. Ferguson.*

On June 7, 1892, Homer Adolph Plessy bought a ticket in New Orleans, Louisiana, to go to Covington, Louisiana, and boarded an East Louisiana Railroad passenger train. Plessy was a member of the Negro aristocracy in New Orleans, citizens of culture, education and considerable wealth, who had enjoyed freedom from slavery for several generations. Many of the group had French names, as a result of intermarriage with the old-line French families which had founded the city.

Even more than the recently freed slaves, the Negro aristocracy of New Orleans was appalled by the wave of anti-Negro feeling which swept over the country in the 1880s. They particularly objected to the Jim Crow laws being passed in the former Confederate states. Louisiana had on July 10, 1890, passed a law requiring railroads "to provide equal but separate accommodations for the white and colored races." From that day on, trains in Louisiana—and in most other Southern and border states—had a car for Negroes and a car for whites.

New Orleans' Negro leadership sought to test the constitutionality of the law and sent Plessy to sit in the white coach. This act caused no stir, because Plessy was, by his own admission, seven-eighths white and one-eighth Negro. He looked white or, as *Plessy v. Ferguson* stated it, "the mixture of colored blood was not discernible in him."

The railroad had rather obviously been alerted to Plessy's invasion and he was asked by the conductor to move to the Jim Crow car. Plessy refused and was arrested by Detective Christopher C. Cain and charged with violation of the Jim Crow law.

Plessy's influential friends had prepared for this day, having employed a most celebrated attorney to defend the case, Albion Winegar Tourgée. History can boast few more colorful characters than Tourgée. He had been the most eminent carpetbagger in the Reconstruction era and a prominent North Carolina leader during that time. He was the author of several highly successful novels. Now he was employed as Plessy's chief counsel.

Plessy was brought before Judge John H. Ferguson of the Criminal District Court for the Parish of New Orleans, where Tourgée claimed the law was unconstitutional. Plessy lost and eventually, as intended, the case went to the Supreme Court, where Justice Henry Billings Brown rendered the opinion for the 7-1 majority that separate but equal facilities for Negroes were constitutional.

Read today, Justice Brown's opinion has, for many people, the stench of racism in it. Its logic is disheveled and its views now appear disreputable. But you must remember that in 1896 it reflected the prevailing opinion of the times. It is probable the Court was reflecting the "dominant opinion" of the period. For its time, *Plessy v. Ferguson* was a milestone in the path of Negro rights. While it upheld segregation, it also clearly draped the equal-protection clause of the Fourteenth Amendment around the Negro.

"The object of the Fourteenth Amendment," said Justice Brown, "was undoubtedly to enforce the absolute equality of the two races before the law, but in the nature of things it would not have been intended to abolish distinctions based upon color or to enforce social, as distinguished from political equality, or a commingling of the two races upon terms unsatisfactory to either. Laws permitting or even requiring their separateness in places where they are liable to be brought into contact do not necessarily imply the inferiority of either race to the other."

Justice Brown then spoke *obiter dicta*—that is, he "dragged in from left field" another issue which had nothing to do with Jim Crow on public transportation. He said: "The most common instance of this [segregation] is connected with the establishment of separate schools for white and colored children, which has been held to be a valid exercise of the legislative powers even by the courts of states where the rights of the colored race have been longest and most earnestly enforced. . . . We cannot say that a law which authorizes or even requires the separation of the two races in public conveyances is unreasonable or more obnoxious to the Fourteenth Amendment than the acts of Congress requiring separate schools for colored children in the District of Columbia, the constitutionality of which does not seem to have been questioned, or the corresponding acts of state legislature."

Under the law, Justice Brown's *obiter dicta* about school segregation did not have the force of law—technically, that is—but it remained law for more half of the twentieth century.

Then Justice Brown got to the heart of his argument: "We consider the underlying fallacy of the plaintiff's [Plessy] argument to consist in the assumption that the enforced separation of the two races stamps the colored race with the badge of inferiority. If this is so, it is not by reason of anything found in the act, but solely because the colored race chooses to put that construction upon it. . . . The argument also assumes that social prejudices may be overcome by legislation, and that equal rights cannot be secured by Negroes except by an enforced commingling of the two races. We cannot accept this proposition. . . . Legislation is powerless to eradicate racial instincts, or to abolish distinctions based upon physical differences, and the attempt to do so can only result in accentuating the difficulties of the present situation. If the civil and political rights of both races be equal, one cannot be inferior to the other civilly or politically. If one race be inferior to the other socially, the Constitution of the United States cannot put them upon the same plane."

From a legal standpoint, the Court's opinion lacks merit. The principal legal precedent was a case which occurred before the Civil War and the adoption of the Fourteenth Amendment. For the most part, *Plessy v. Ferguson* wrote the prevailing sociological and psychological opinions of the day into law.

But there was a unique opinion given in *Plessy v. Ferguson*, the dissent of Justice John Marshall Harlan, grandfather of the present Justice of the same name. Justice Harlan was a remarkable man in his age, a former slaveholder who became the foremost advocate of Negro rights in his time. His advocacy bore rich fruit in this dissent:

"The arbitrary separation of citizens, on the basis of race, while they are on a public highway, is a badge of servitude wholly inconsistent with the civil freedom and the equality before the law established by the Constitution. It cannot be justified upon any legal grounds. . . .

"But in view of the Constitution, in the eye of the law, there is in this country no superior, no dominant, ruling class of citizens. There is no caste here. Our Constitution is color-blind, and neither knows nor tolerates classes among citizens. In respect of civil rights, all citizens are equal before the law. The humblest is the peer of the most powerful. The law regards man as man and takes no account of his surroundings or of his color when his civil rights as guaranteed by the supreme law of the land are involved. . . . We boast of the freedom enjoyed by our people above all other peoples. But it is difficult to reconcile that boast with a state of law which, practically, puts the brand of servitude and degradation upon a large class of our fellow citizens—our equals before the law. The thin disguise of "equal" accommodations for passengers in railroad coaches will not mislead anyone, nor atone for the wrong this day done.

"The present decision, it may well be apprehended, will not only stimulate aggressions, more or less brutal and irritating, upon the admitted rights of colored citizens, but will encourage the belief that it is possible, by means of state enactments, to defeat the beneficent purposes which the people of the United States had in view when they adopted the recent amendments of the Constitution. . . . In my opinion, the judgment this day rendered will, in time, prove to be quite as pernicious as the decision made by this tribunal in the *Dred Scott* case."

Few men have had the misfortune to be so prophetic, yet in 1938 when Thurgood Marshall and the legal staff of the NAACP declared war on racial segregation in schools and other places, *Plessy v. Ferguson* was the citadel of prejudice barring their way.

Marshall and his staff assaulted the fortress on several legal fronts. It was slow, tiresome work, preparing briefs and oral arguments and rearguments, first in one court and then another—and waiting and waiting for the case to be heard and for decision to be made. For a race of Americans awaiting the freedom supposedly won for them on Civil War battlefields, the progress could hardly have been slower. World War II came and the nation's energies were put to tasks of greater urgency than civil rights. But, however slowly, progress was made.

In 1944 the Supreme Court decided *Smith v. Allwright* (321 U.S. 649) affecting the Negro's right to vote. The Fifteenth Amendment supposedly guaranteed the Negro the right to vote, but states had become expert in denying that vote by legal tricks. One was to allow Negroes to vote in general elections but not in primaries. Since most

Southern states were solidly Democratic and for practical purposes had only a one-party system, the primary vote was the important one because condidates reflecting the white power structure were elected to appear on the ballot for the general election. Negroes were thus effectively disenfranchised. Since the Court felt the primary an intergal part of the election process, they overruled an earlier decision and declared "white primaries" unconstitutional. While this case hardly settled Negro voting-rights questions, it was progress.

Jim Crow laws affecting public transportation were attacked by Marshall. In 1941 the Court, in *Mitchell v. United States* (316 U.S. 702), ordered the desegregation of Pullman facilities on railroads. A key, Marshall-led case came in 1945. For many years, if a Negro boarded an interstate bus in a Northern city—say, New York—and headed south, he was allowed to sit wherever he wished. At the border of a Southern state the bus stopped and the passengers were reseated Jim Crow style. It was a case of Negroes please move to the rear.

Marshall did not attack the illegality of segregation on these bus trips. He was still unwilling to risk everything on an effort to have segregation declared unconstitutional. Instead, he attacked the practice on the ground that requiring buses to stop at the Virginia border and to reseat the passengers was an impediment to interstate commerce.

At that time the Supreme Court was deciding interstate-commerce cases by weighing the benefit the state received from its regulation against the burden it imposed on the transportation firms. In *Morgan v. Virginia* (328 U.S. 373), the benefit-burden principle was applied to segregation on interstate buses. The burden surely was small. It took only a moment or two for the bus to stop and passengers to reseat themselves. A bus might linger longer at a red light. Yet, the Court, in an opinion by Justice Stanley F. Reed, held that even this negligible burden outweighed the benefit. This could mean only that there was no recognized benefit in segregated seating, none at all.

In 1950 the Court voided segregation in dining cars on trains, and in 1955 the Interstate Commerce Commission struck the fatal blow to Jim Crow by ordering complete desegregation of all interstate transportation facilities in the country.

A major move against prejudice came in the matter of housing. Marshall and the NAACP asked the Court to rule against restrictive covenants. This was a system of private arrangements whereby everyone buying a house in a "restricted" neighborhood or development was required to sign an agreement that he would not sell to persons of certain ancestries, usually Negroes and Jews. If the homeowner tried to sell to "undesirables," his neighbors could obtain a court order to enforce the agreement and block the sale.

In this case, *Shelley v. Kraemer* (334 U.S. 1), the Court made one of its more important, far-reaching and controversial decisions. Restrictive agreements themselves are not unconstitutional, the Court ruled in an opinion by Chief Justice Fred Vinson, but they cannot be enforced in state courts. In other words, a homeowner could sign such an agreement if he wished, but his neighbors could not go to court to force him to live up to it, for a court order constituted state action in support of discrimination and, hence, violated the Fourteenth Amendment. A decade and a half later, this case would take on great significance as the Court wrestled with difficult problems stemming from racial discrimination in restaurants, motels and other public places.

As we have seen, by 1950 the legal staff of the NAACP had made a little progress in breaching the walls of prejudice. Separate but equal was still the law of the land—particularly in education. Thurgood Marshall's work still lay ahead of him.

IV. A WRONG IS RIGHTED

> . . . *In the field of public education the doctrine of "separate but equal" has no place. Separate educational facilities are inherently unequal.*—Chief Justice Earl Warren for the Court in BROWN V. BOARD OF EDUCATION OF TOPEKA

If you were Charles Houston and Thurgood Marshall in the mid-1930s and hoped to end school segregation in the United States, how would you go about it?

One method, which was considered for a time, was to flood Southern states with a series of taxpayers' suits against elementary and high-school segregation. This, some maintained, would force the Southern states to forego segregated schools as impossibly expensive.

This approach was abandoned in favor of a series of court actions to force Southern universities to admit Negroes to their graduate and professional schools. The first reason for using this method was that post-graduate schools, particularly law schools, were the weakest link in the segregation armor. Southern states went through the motions, at least, of providing separate but equal educational facilities for elementary and high-school students, but they had no Negro law and other professional schools.

The NAACP lawyers hoped that if the Southern states attempted to develop separate but equal law schools, they would find it so expensive they would end segregation in all white professional schools.

This indirect approach to the problem of school segregation exploited a peculiarity of Southern racial prejudice—that is, that "commingling of the races" is somehow less desirable when the children are younger than when they are older. As Marshall put it, "Those racial supremacy boys somehow think that little kids of six or seven are going to get funny ideas about sex and marriage just from going to school together, but for some equally funny reasons youngsters in law school aren't supposed to feel that way. We didn't get it, but we decided that if that is what the South believed, then the best thing for the moment was to go along."

A victory was not long in coming. The Supreme Court ruled in 1938 that refusal by the University of Missouri to admit a Negro named Gaines to its law school constituted a violation of the equal-protection clause of the Fourteenth Amendment. Missouri, since it had no law school for Negroes, followed the usual practice and offered to pay Gaines's tuition at a desegregated law school in the North. The Court refused to accept this system, pointing out that "a privilege has been created for white law students which is denied to Negroes."

The NAACP's victory in this case was a hollow one. Gaines failed to take advantage of his educational opportunity and mysteriously disappeared. No one else stepped forward to use the hard-won privilege. Few qualified Negro graduate and professional students seem to have been interested in equal educational opportunities at that time.

The next school-desegregation victory for Marshall was ten years in the making, but in 1948, in *Sipuel v. Board of Regents* (332 U.S. 631), the high court unanimously denied an Oklahoma attempt to deny a Negro admission to the state university school of law. This decision was similar to the Gaines case, but its effect was more far-reaching. After the decision, the Oklahoma Board of Regents, which governs the state university, voted to admit Negroes to any course of study not provided in the State College for Negroes. This was admission that the separate-but-equal doctrine was unworkable at the graduate-school level. "You can't build a cyclotron for one student," University of Oklahoma President George L. Cross was said to have remarked at the time.

A little to the south, in Austin, Texas, educators were not convinced of the accuracy of President Cross's statement and sought, in a spectacular way, to circumvent the Oklahoma ruling. The case began when a Houston mail carrier named Sweatt sought admission to the University of Texas law school at Houston. Denied entry, he sought relief in the state courts. The state Supreme Court, instead of requiring Sweatt's admission, ordered the university to furnish Sweatt with "substantially equal" facilities. The university promptly created a Negro law school and invited Sweatt to attend. This activity was both applauded and condemned by university students, who held mass meetings to dramatize their viewpoints.

Sweatt refused to attend and again petitioned for admission to the white law school. Marshall, representing Sweatt, paraded legal and academic experts to the witness stand to testify that the fly-by-night Negro law school was in no way comparable to that for the white Texans. Climax came when Robert Redfield, distinguished University of Chicago anthropologist, testified that science no longer believed there were inherent differences betwen Negroes and whites. The Texas Supreme Court was unimpressed, however, and ruled against Sweatt.

In 1950 the Supreme Court Justices ruled on *Sweatt v. Painter* (339 U.S. 629). They had received a brief submitted by 150 law professors stating that the Constitution did not condone segregation at all and that segregated legal education could never be equal. Chief Justice Vinson ridiculed the alleged equality of the Negro school and said, "It is difficult to believe that one who had a free choice between these law schools would consider the question [of which was the better] closed." Sweatt was ordered admitted to the regular law school—where he promptly flunked. Nevertheless, the meaning of "equal" in "separate but equal" had been clarified.

On the same day the Court ruled in the *Sweatt* case, the Justices held that it was unconstitutional for the University of Oklahoma to compel Negro students to sit in a roped-off section of the classroom marked "reserved for colored." In his opinion in *McLaurin v. Oklahoma Regents* (339 U.S. 637), Chief Justice Vinson said such practices "handicapped" the student in pursuing "effective graduate instruction."

In 1950 the NAACP's campaign to desegregate schools seemed to be a failure. Expensive hard-fought court battles had won admission for a handful of graduate students to white schools. At this rate, several centuries would pass before the mass of Negro elementary and high-school students were allowed to attend the same schools as white children.

Worse, all of Marshall's efforts appeared to have the effect of strengthening the separate-but-equal rule of *Plessy v. Ferguson*. The *McLaurin, Sweatt* and *Sipuel* decisions were based on the inadequacy of the segregated schools. If the South could maintain substantially equal segregated facilities, it seemed the Court would not interfere.

Yet, the NAACP had put much testimony into the record that segregated graduate schools were inherently unequal, that separate facilities were discriminatory and that discrimination handicapped a student's learning. Even more, the Court's decisions of the last decade in school, transportation and housing matters indicated it was against segregation. Was the Court now ready to discard the old separate-but-equal rule and declare all segregation in public life unconstitutional?

In 1950 the NAACP began its legal assault on the *Plessy v. Ferguson* fortress with five carefully selected cases around the country.

In Clarendon County, South Carolina, in a case which became known as *Briggs v. Elliott*, Negro children in elementary and high schools brought action in the United States District Court for the Eastern District of South Carolina to stop enforcement of the state constitution and state laws requiring segregation of Negroes. A three-judge panel found that Negro schools were inferior and ordered the state to begin immediately to equalize them. The judges ruled, however, that the state laws and constitution were valid in their enforcement of segregation if the facilities were equal. The district judges denied the Negro children the right to attend the white schools while the equalization program was taking place. This case went to the Supreme Court, which sent it back to the district court for a progress report on the equalization program. The lower court found that substantial equality had been achieved between the Negro and white school systems, except for school buildings, and progress was being made there. The case then returned to the Supreme Court for decisions on the constitutional questions.

In Prince Edward County, Virginia, the case being labeled *Davis v. County School Board*, a group of Negro high-school students asked the U.S. District Court for the Eastern District of Virginia to stop enforcement of the state constitution and state laws requiring segregation. A three-judge district-court panel denied the request, but found Negro schools to be inferior in physical plant, curriculum and teacher training, and ordered the defendants to correct the situation.

In New Castle County, Delaware—the case of *Gebhart v. Belton* —the NAACP attorneys brought action in the Delaware Court of Chancery on behalf of Negro elementary and high-school students to enjoin enforcement of segregation laws. The chancellor (judge) of the state court ruled in favor of the Negro children and ordered their immediate admission to the white schools. The state court maintained that the Negro schools were inferior in teacher training, pupil-teacher ratio, extracurricular activities, physical plant and time and distance children had to travel to school. The chancellor also found that segregation itself resulted in an inferior education for Negro children, but he did not base his decision on that ground.

The chancellor's decision was appealed to the State Supreme Court, where it was upheld, except that the high state court ruled that once Negro schools were made equal, the court's order might be modified so that the Negro children would have to return to a segregated status.

The fourth case was in Topeka, Kansas, where litigation was brought in behalf of eleven-year-old Linda Brown and other Negro children. The petition asked the United States District Court for Kansas to enjoin enforcement of a Kansas statute which permitted, but did not require, cities of more than 15,000 population to maintain separate school facilities for Negroes and whites. In accordance with that law, the Topeka Board of Education had established segregated elementary schools. All other schools were nonsegregated.

The three-judge Federal District Court in Kansas found that

segregation has a bad effect on Negro children but denied the petition on the ground that Negro and white schools were substantially equal.

These four cases, coming from the East, South and West, charged that segregation violated the equal-protection clause of the Fourteenth Amendment. The fifth case from the District of Columbia charged that segregation in the nation's capital violated the due-process clause of the Fifth Amendment. This same clause—that no man shall be "deprived of life, liberty or property without due process of law"—was the same constitutional provision Chief Justice Taney had used in the *Dred Scott* case to rule slavery legal.

In December 1952 all five cases came before the Supreme Court. For the NAACP there were Marshall, Nabrit, Louis Redding, Greenberg and others. For the defendants there was John W. Davis, a distinguished constitutional lawyer and 1924 Democratic Presidential candidate. Edward T. McGranahan, then the Attorney General, asked the Court to declare school segregation invalid under the equal-protection clause. Thirty social scientists supplied opinion and information on the psychic damage segregation does to both Negro and white children.

Six months later, in June 1953, the Justices set the case for reargument and asked the counsel for both sides to answer a series of historical questions dealing with the original intent of the framers of the Fourteenth Amendment. In short, the Justices asked if the framers intended or had any notion that the Amendment might be used to abolish school segregation.

Marshall, in what he has described as " the smartest move I ever made in my life," called in historians, social scientists and constitutional experts to research the historical questions asked by the Court. They found considerable evidence to support a contention that the framers of the Amendment indeed had in mind its being used to desegregate schools.

A great deal of effort went into this historical research and the legal reasoning Marshall should take. On November 15, 1953, the NAACP filed its formal brief or argument in *Brown v. Board of Education of Topeka,* contending "it was the intent of the proponents of the Fourteenth Amendment that it could, of its own force, prohibit all state action based upon race or color" and "all segregation in public education." The brief argued that *Plessy v. Ferguson* had been "conceived in error."

The briefs filed by the various boards of education cited considerable historical evidence that the Fourteenth Amendment was not intended to undo school segregation. South Carolina argued in behalf of states' rights. Virginia said reversal of *Plessy v. Ferguson* would "overthrow the established meaning of the Fourteenth Amendment." Kansas disliked "federal interference" in state schools.

Oral argument was heard on December 8, 1953. Marshall and Spottswood Robinson III, having prepared in rehearsals in which nine-member panels of law professors fired questions at them as they believed the Justices would, made their argument. Davis made a compelling presentation that *Plessy v. Ferguson* should not be set aside for sociological reasons. There were many questions from the Justices.

On May 19, 1964, Anthony Lewis, a reporter for the New York *Times*, recalled the events of a decade earlier, specifically May 17, 1954. "Shortly after noon . . ." Mr. Lewis recalled, "reporters waiting in the Supreme Court press room for what they thought would be a routine opinion were suddenly told to go to the courtroom. There Chief Justice Earl Warren was reading his opinion for the court in Case No. 1 on the docket that term, *Brown v. Board of Education of Topeka*. For minutes the audience listened without indication of the outcome, then the Chief Justice read, "We come then to the question presented. Does segregation of children in public schools solely on the basis of race, even though the physical facilities and other tangible factors may be equal, deprive the child of the minority group of equal educational opportunities. We believe that it does."

Today when you enter a law library and pick up the 347th volume of Supreme Court decisions and turn to page 483 to read *Brown v. Board*, as it is usually abbreviated, a hush seems to fall over the room. The words composed by Chief Justice Warren are simple, lucid, nonlegal and most understandable. The opinion is brief, only eleven pages long—all of which gives it the flavor and tone of a great historical document. The Constitution itself, the Declaration of Independence, the Gettysburg Address are simple and concise.

The Chief Justice said the "plaintiffs contend that segregated public schools are not 'equal' and cannot be made 'equal' and that hence they are deprived of the equal protection of the law." He then dispensed with all the work of the historians on the intent of the framers of the Fourteenth Amendment in one sentence, saying the evidence was "at best . . . inconclusive."

He continued: "In approaching this problem, we cannot turn the clock back to 1868 when the Amendment was adopted or even to 1896 when *Plessy v. Ferguson* was written. We must consider public education in the light of its full development and its present place in American life throughout the nation. Only in this way can it be determined if segregation in public schools deprives the plaintiffs of the equal protection of the laws."

Chief Justice Warren then said how important education is, calling it the "foundation of good citizenship," and posed the question already quoted—that is, does segregation itself deprive a minority of equal educational opportunity? His answer: "We believe that it does."

"To separate them from others of similar age and qualifications solely because of their race generates a feeling of inferiority as to their status in the community that may affect their hearts and minds in a way unlikely ever to be undone. . . . We conclude that in the field of public education the doctrine of 'separate but equal' has no place. Separate educational facilities are inherently unequal."

Fifty-eight years to the day later, the Supreme Court had unanimously reversed *Plessy v. Ferguson*.

Technically speaking, *Brown v. Board* covered the cases from Kansas, Virginia, South Carolina and Delaware. The District of Columbia case, *Bolley v. Sharpe*, was settled separately, with Mr. Warren writing for a unanimous Court that segregation also violates the due-process clause of the Fifth Amendment. The Court did not decide on that historic day in 1954 the thorny problems of how desegregation should be effected. The cases were all sent back to the district court for hearing on the matter of implementation. The cases returned to the Supreme Court, and on May 31, 1955, the Court declined to order immediate desegregation but urged "all deliberate speed" in bringing it to pass.

The political, social and economic repercussions of *Brown v.*

Board may well be unsurpassed in our history and will be discussed in the following chapter. At this point it must be said, however, that few decisions in court history have been so denounced or so praised. Southern politicians in particular leaped to abuse the Court for the decision—and more, to abuse the Justices in general and the Chief Justice in particular for making the decision. The Court's action was quickly seen by critics as a diabolical scheme to undermine the American way of life.

As was observed in the opening chapter, this chorus of denunciation of the Supreme Court has continued largely unabated for over a decade. Much of it, including the palavar about pro-Communism and cries for impeachment of the Chief Justice, has to be dismissed as drivel. Not to be taken lightly, however, are the views of legal, historical and social critics. Their criticism has been so constant for so many years that it is difficult to keep abreast of it, let alone digest it in a book of this sort.

An excellent attempt to do so was made in the April 1956 issue of the American Bar Association *Journal,* a publication by and for the legal profession. The *Journal's* editors sought to print articles "fairly representative" of the views of both sides of the *Brown v. Board* controversy. Speaking in opposition to the Court ruling were co-authors Eugene Cook, Attorney General of Georgia, and William I. Potter of Kansas City, Missouri.

They blasted the Warren opinion on the grounds that it was a "radical departure from the doctrine of *stare decisis*" [that is, that previous decisions of the courts should stand] and that the Court, without an Act of Congress, has assumed the power to enforce "commingling of the white and colored races," thus nullifying state laws and further encroaching on states' rights.

In ringing tones the authors denounced the Warren opinion:

"Absent from the opinion was reference to the effect on the hearts and minds of white children and their parents because of enforced commingling with Negro children. . . .

"In rendering its decision, the Supreme Court rejected the traditional rule of constitutional construction and substituted the intent of the Court for the intent of the people. . . .

"No longer is there a question of whether there exists a conflict with precedent or whether precedent is wrong, but rather whether

the intent of the framers as recognized in previous decisions is, in
the opinion of the judges, 'outmoded.'

"In its decision, the Supreme Court did not hold the old separate
but equal doctrine . . . was bad law. It held that it was bad sociology. It did not hold that the facts (or truth) described in the
records in the cases before the Court justified a departure from the
separate but equal doctrine. It held that 'psychological knowledge'
apart from these records was of more validity than the factual truth.

". . . great harm will result when a social scientist takes his
deduction and generalizations into the field of judicial interpretation
and treats them as . . . 'law.'

"In its singlemindedness and preoccupation in seeking to justify a
radically new construction of the equal-protection clause of the
Fourteenth Amendment so as to outlaw state segregation of schools,
it by-passed and overrode the much greater constitutional principle
that the people are sovereign, that the national government has only
specific powers delegated to it by the Constitution and that all other
powers reside in the states and in the people."

The article by Cook and Potter places great emphasis on the fact
that the Chief Justice used nonlegal, sociological and psychological
authorities to justify the conclusion that segregation is harmful to
children. They impugned the reputations of the cited authorities as
having subversive affiliations.

The immediate reply to this article came from George W. Stum-
berg, professor of law at the University of Texas. He said it was "un-
lawyer-like" to refer to a decision as "unlawful" and "invalid." He
noted that the principle of judicial review—that is, for the Supreme
Court to decide whether state laws are constitutional—is "so thoroughly imbedded in our system of government that for it now to
become otherwise, a constitutional amendment or a revolution
would be necessary, neither of which is likely to occur."

A better defense of the Court came in the same journal on June
1957 in an article by George L. DeLacy, former president of the
Omaha and Nebraska Bar Associations. "It occurs to me," he wrote,
"that the Supreme Court of the United States, when presented with
the specific question involved, could not, in the light of its previous
decisions in the *Sweatt* case and *McLaurin* case and in the light of
modern thinking on the subject, have held otherwise."

DeLacy wrote: "The Supreme Court was presented with the proposition of whether furnishing separate but equal facilities for education was a violation of the Fourteenth Amendment. It could not equivocate. It had to hold that it was or was not a deprivation of the equal rights of the Negro citizens as guaranteed by the Amendment. . . . In my opinion this was a judicial question and it not at all evidenced any intent upon the part of the Supreme Court to legislate. . . . The Supreme Court had this duty to determine whether or not there was a violation of the Fourteenth Amendment and this is all it did." A point of interest which seems to lessen DeLacy's point is that in earlier cases the Court explicitly refused to consider the question of segregation as an evil *per se*.

But the Court's opinion in *Brown v. Board* should hardly have come as a surprise to anyone in the legal profession. The rulings over the preceding fifteen years in *Sweatt, McLaurin, Sipuel, Shelley v. Kraemer, Morgan v. Virginia* and other cases pointed toward a gradually increasing psychological awareness that there would be an eventual outlawing of school segregation. The actions of universities in admitting Negro students and in local boards of education in improving the standards of education for Negroes indicated the awareness of the necessary course of events.

Furthermore, these earlier segregation cases going back to 1938 are ample precedent for the *Brown v. Board* ruling. The criticism that the Court abruptly reversed *Plessy v. Ferguson* is unfair and historically unsound.

The argument that the Court based its opinion on sociological thinking is not well taken either. There were legal precedents, but even if there hadn't been there is nothing unusual in basing opinions on sociological concepts. *Plessy v. Ferguson* is based, as the lawyers say, on bad law and sociology. It wrote the prevailing social opinions of the day into law.

Where *Brown v. Board* may be criticized—which is not to say whether the criticism is right or wrong—is that it encroached on states' rights and usurped the powers of Congress and state legislatures. But even these arguments are weakened by the unanimity of the Court. Among those voting for the decision was a former Alabama Senator, Hugo L. Black, and a Texas politician, Tom C. Clark. In agreement were the foremost exponents of judicial activism, Justice Black and Justice Douglas, and that towering advocate of judicial restraint, Justice Frankfurter.

With each passing year the criticisms of *Brown v. Board* seem less and less well taken and the decision appears to be of a high order in legal stature and logic, as well as in humanitarian and historical importance.

V. THE LAW BECOMES
COLOR-BLIND

The Supreme Court "never contemplated that the concept of deliberate speed would countenance indefinite delay in elimination of racial barriers in schools."—Justice Arthur J. Goldberg

On the tenth anniversary of the Supreme Court's school-desegregation decision, reporters sought out Thurgood Marshall in his offices in Foley Square, New York. This was a different location than formerly, for in 1961 President John F. Kennedy had named Marshall to be judge of the United States Circuit Court of Appeals for the Second District in New York. Judge Marshall had distinguished himself as special counsel to the NAACP, arguing thirty-two cases before the Supreme Court and winning twenty-nine. He turned out to be as good a judge as a lawyer, writing more than 100 opinions, none of which were reversed by the Supreme Court. Several of his dissents became law.

Now, in May 1964, Judge Marshall was being asked his opinions about the results of the hard-fought *Brown v. Board* case. Although he was heavier and grayer, Judge Marshall's manner of speaking had lost little of its informality. "Obviously," he told the reporters, "desegregation hasn't proceeded as fast as many of us would like."

The trouble, he said, was the May 31, 1955, opinion of the Court allowing school desegregation to occur with "all deliberate speed."

Said Judge Marshall: "If you look in Webster's you'll see that either the first or second definition for 'deliberate' means 'slow.' It means don't rush it, don't proceed without reason. We wanted it [the Supreme Court] to say immediately."

Judge Marshall then recalled that he and Roy Wilkins, head of the NAACP, had appeared at a press conference the day after the 1955 court order. "Roy Wilkins and I said we were perfectly satisfied with the opinion, but the picture of us in the paper made it look like we had lost our best friend, and I think that was the way it was."

"All deliberate speed." Ten years after the Supreme Court decision, the New York *Times* surveyed schools in the six border states and eleven former Confederate states to determine progress in racial desegregation. In the border states 55 per cent of the 514,000 Negro school children were attending desegregated schools, indicating considerable progress and the great value of the Court's decision in bringing about desegregation.

However, in the former Confederate states "deliberateness" has never been so slow. At the start of the second decade under the Supreme Court edict, only 34,110 Negro children out of 2,890,000— or 1.18 per cent—were attending desegregated classes. The best record was in Texas, where 5.52 per cent of the Negroes were integrated; the poorest record was in intransigent Mississippi, where not one Negro child was going to school with a white child.

This situation led Arthur J. Goldberg, when he was an Associate Justice of the Supreme Court, to comment, "*Brown* never contemplated that the concept of deliberate speed would countenance indefinite delay in elimination of racial barriers in schools."

Such progress as has been made in the Deep South has been marked by almost incomprehensible violence. No attempt will be made here to provide a complete record, only to recall a few of the events that made headlines: September 1957, federal troops march into Little Rock to protect Negro high-school students attending Central High; April 1962, federal troops sent to the University of Mississippi at Oxford after race riots involving student James Meredith's admission; Medgar W. Evers, Mississippi state field secretary of the NAACP, assassinated outside his Jackson, Mississippi, home; Maryland National Guard dispatched to Cambridge, Maryland, to maintain law and order; rioting, bombing and arson accompany admission of Negroes to four white public schools in Alabama; four Negro girls killed and twenty-three persons injured in the dynamiting of a Birmingham church and two Negro boys killed by gunfire in violence that followed; Birmingham home of Negro lawyer bombed twice in fifteen days, touching off violence in which Negro man was shot and killed; desegregated high school burned; riots force Chester, Pennsylvania, to close schools temporarily.

The complete list would include the murder of four civil-rights workers near Philadelphia, Mississippi; the murder of a Detroit housewife in Alabama; race riots in New York City; Rochester, New York; Los Angeles, California; and many, many others.

But perhaps the most illuminating evidence of failure to desegregate schools may be found in the original cases brought by the NAACP. In Clarendon County, South Carolina, ten years after *Brown v. Board,* not one Negro child attended a white school. The second Southern target, you will recall, was Prince Edward County, Virginia, which closed down its public-school system in 1959 rather than desegregate, an action which was finally declared unconstitutional by the Supreme Court in 1964, a decade after *Brown v. Board.*

Such a record would seem to indicate that the school-desegregation decision was unimportant. Actually, its importance is immeasurable, because it was one of the sparks that ignited what has come to be called the "Negro revolution" in America. *Brown v. Board* cut away some of the legal and moral underpinnings which had shored up white supremacy in America. *Brown v. Board* gave Negro leadership the courage and determination to demand true equality of citizenship, complete acceptance into the American way of life, an end to second-class citizenship for all Negroes. *Brown v. Board* aroused the conscience of white Americans, making them aware that racism is racism whether practiced in Nazi Germany or in the "land of liberty." It made America conscious of the unexamined myths which had gripped the nation for a century.

True, there were many factors other than *Brown v. Board* that led to the Negro revolution. Millions of Negroes and whites had fought side by side in World War II and the Korean conflict, breaking down traditional racial barriers. The increased industrialization and urbanization of the South had broadened traditional, narrow, rural thinking. Mass communication, particularly by television, had undermined old-line regional provincialism and made us conscious that we are one nation and one people.

Yet it was *Brown v. Board* which lit the fuse to the revolution, and it was the young, liberal college students, both white and Negro, who were the revolutionaries. This book cannot hope even to begin to trace the history of this revolution, but the use of sit-ins, walk-ins, lie-ins, ride-ins and a host of other "ins," as well as public demonstrations and protests of a wide variety, dramatized the discrimination and created pressure on public officials to correct the abuse. The street demonstrations also provoked counterviolence, the so-called "white backlash." The record in many places is written in blood and riots, burnings and bombings.

The street demonstrations and the mass arrests of hundreds of persons at a time as tests of segregation laws meant that many of the revolution's battles were fought in the courts of the nation. It is this aspect of it that we are most concerned about in this book.

The Negro's goal of complete acceptance into American life has involved two major elements—school desegregation where progress has been limited, and discrimination against Negroes in public accommodations, employment, housing, elections, entertainment and all other aspects of life. Of these, the greatest energy has gone toward winning the Negro admission to public accommodations.

This is hardly a new fight, nor are the techniques being used by civil-rights workers today. What is fairly new is racial discrimination. In the beginning and for the first 250 years of slavery in America, the Negro, particularly in cities, was accepted. He rode on trains and streetcars without Jim Crow laws. He was seated in restaurants and sold lodgings in inns and hotels without hesitation—in both the South and the North. To forestall mounting post-Civil War discrimination, the Civil Rights Act of 1866 guaranteed Negroes the equal benefit of the laws. Many court suits were brought to test denial of the use of public accommodations to Negroes. Most state and federal rulings between 1865 and 1880 were in favor of the Negro. Racial discrimination was far from a fixture in American life.

Negroes of that era also used means other than legal ones to win their rights—methods commonplace today. In 1871 Negroes in

Louisville, Kentucky, conducted what we would today term a "ride-in" to win seats on horse-drawn streetcars. The transportation company had a policy requiring Negroes to stand on the open platforms in front of the cars. If a Negro took a seat, the car didn't move until he stood up. Negroes launched a campaign to change this. They paid their nickel fare and took a seat. They continued to sit, while the streetcar remained stationary and rednecks hurled insults at them. After considerable disorder, the trolley company rescinded its policy.

Despite civil-rights test cases, many localities, particularly in the South, passed segregation laws or developed discriminatory practices. While most courts held these laws and practices to be invalid, a substantial minority of courts ruled that Negroes could be denied use of public accommodations. To settle the issue, Congress passed the Civil Rights Act of March 1, 1875, which declared that "all persons within the jurisdiction of the United States shall be entitled to the full and equal enjoyment of the accommodations . . . of inns, public conveyances on land or water, theaters and other places of public amusement; subject only to the conditions and limitations established by law, and applicable alike to citizens of every race or color." The law also has a penalty provision carrying fines up to $1,000 and thirty-day jail sentences.

Such was the law on November 22, 1879, when William R. Davis, Jr., twenty-six, business agent for a weekly newspaper, accompanied by his girl friend, whom the newspapers described as "a bright octoroon, almost white," bought two seats to a matinee performance at the Grand Opera House in New York City. He wanted to see Edwin Booth, the celebrated actor, in Victor Hugo's *Ruy Blas*. Davis bought tickets, but when he presented them at the entrance the doorkeeper, Samuel Singleton said, "These tickets are no good." Davis' money was refunded.

Davis went outside and paid a white youth to go to the boxoffice to buy him two tickets. This was done, and when Davis again tried to enter, Singleton once more refused him. Davis filed a criminal complaint, and on December 9, Singleton was indicted. At his trial on January 14, 1880, Singleton, through his attorney, Louis Post, claimed that the Civil Rights Act of 1875, under which he had been indicted, was unconstitutional. The district court referred the constitutional question to the circuit court, whose two judges disagreed on the matter. The case then reached the Supreme Court as *U.S. v. Singleton* in 1880, along with five other similar tests of the 1875 law. Lumped together, the cases form the celebrated *Civil Rights Cases* (109 U.S. 3), decided October 15, 1883.

Justice Joseph Bradley, speaking for the Court, agreed that the Thirteenth Amendment forbade slavery and involuntary servitude, but that it could not be stretched to cover "social" discrimination such as that being inflicted on Davis. As for the Fourteenth Amendment, it controlled state actions and did not govern private acts of discrimination, such as that Singleton was carrying out for owners of the Grand Opera House. Neither Amendment gave Congress, Justice Bradley held, the power to control private actions as it did in the act of 1875. Therefore, the act was unconstitutional. Justice Bradley went on to argue that there must be some point at which the Negro ceased to be "the special favorite of the law" and took on "the rank of mere citizens."

The decision in the *Civil Rights Cases* was the death knell for the Negro efforts to thwart discrimination against him in public places, just as *Plessy v. Ferguson,* thirteen years later, relegated him to a largely segregated existence.

As he was to do in *Plessy v. Ferguson,* Justice John Marshall Harlan authored a rebuking dissent, arguing that the 1875 Act was constitutional on any of several grounds, and then said: "Today, it is the colored race which is denied, by corporations and individuals wielding public authority, rights fundamental to their freedom and citizenship. At some future time, it may be that some other race will fall under the ban of race discrimination. If the constitutional amendments be enforced, according to the intent with which, as I conceive, they were adopted, there cannot be in this republic, any class of human beings in practical subjection to another class."

At this writing, the decision of the *Civil Rights Cases* is still the law of the land. It has never been overruled. Congress in 1964 again passed a law outlawing discrimination against Negroes using public accommodations. The Supreme Court, at this moment, has agreed to review cases challenging the constitutionality of the law. If the law is upheld, it would finally repeal the 1883 decision.

The decision in effect made discrimination lawful. Those who wished to give vent to personal bigotry could justify their actions by maintaining they were upholding the law of the state and the opinions of the Supreme Court. Prohibiting Negroes from hotels, inns, restaurants, theaters, ball parks, housing developments, assembly rooms and wherever else the public was accommodated became the custom in the North, East and West, as well as in the South.

The sit-ins, lie-ins and other forms of demonstrations and protests of the past decade have been largely aimed at undoing the decision in the *Civil Rights Cases*. The courts have been of great assistance in this effort. In case after case the Supreme Court has struck down state or federal laws or court rulings which attempted to preserve racial segregation on public beaches and bathhouses, municipal golf courses, buses and other forms of public transportation, public parks, athletic events, airport restaurants, municipal auditoriums and other places.

Each of these decisions has been a variation on a common theme—that is, no state shall pass a law discriminating against a person on account of his race. If a white man can play golf on a municipal course or sit on a public bus or play in a public park, so may a Negro, and no state or city or county government shall pass a law preventing him from enjoying the equal protection of the law. This issue has been thoroughly settled.

Equally a matter of law is the fact that the Constitution and its amendments in no way control *private* discrimination. If a man is a bigot and wishes to keep Negroes from entering his private home, there is nothing the law as now written and interpreted by the courts can do to prevent him. Indeed constitutional scholars see no way in which the Constitution could be interpreted to force a man to admit unwanted people to his home or to sit with people he does not want to sit with or to be polite and courteous and friendly and warmhearted. This is private discrimination and, however reprehensible or morally wrong it might be, it is beyond the control of the law and the courts. The hearts of men in a society believing in free speech, free expression and maximum personal liberty are beyond judicial action, and even the Supreme Court must defer to private opinion when it is the dominant opinion.

But if public discrimination is illegal and private discrimination is not, what of that gray line where private and public action overlap?

Suppose you own a restaurant catering to the public. It is private property. You paid for it, you run it and you are responsible. Do you have a right to refuse to serve a Negro simply because he is a Negro?

This is a major unanswered legal question of our times. Sit-ins, ride-ins, lie-ins have been held seeking an answer. Thousands upon thousands of arrests have been made in defense of one view or another. This issue is a judicial confrontation between an irresistible force and an immovable object, civil rights versus property rights. Americans have died by the tens of thousands in defense of individual freedom and in defense of property. Now these two inalienable rights have confronted each other in the 1960s.

The confrontation has not occurred in some remote place, but in cities and towns all across the country wherein Negroes have sought to eat in segregated restaurants and lunchrooms, to sleep in hotels, to watch movies, to ride merry-go-rounds and to use other public accommodations.

Lawyers state the confrontation of civil and property rights in different ways. Professor Monrad G. Paulsen of the Columbia University School of Law has put it this way: "To what extent does the Fourteenth Amendment forbid the states to support private choice, when under the Constitution that choice could not be made by the state itself through its judiciary, its legislature or its executive?" Put in simple language, this means: If no judge, legislature or governor could adopt a rule barring Negroes from places of public accommodation, can a private individual do so?

Problems proliferate from that question, severely challenging the relationship between the citizen and his government, his conscience and his freedom—all of which went before the Supreme Court.

VI. NEW PROBLEMS EMERGE

> *It [the school-segregation decision] merely forbids discrimination. It does not forbid such segregation as occurs as the result of voluntary actions. It merely forbids the use of government power to enforce segregation.*—The so-called "Parker Dictum" of Judge John J. Parker, U.S. Circuit Court of Appeals for the Fourth District

In 1960 between fifteen and twenty Negroes entered Hooper's Restaurant in downtown Baltimore hoping to be served. Hooper's, since moved to a new location to make way for an urban-renewal project, was at that time situated in the hub of downtown Baltimore. It was a popular, busy restaurant, noted for modest prices and good food. As such it was a thriving restaurant and a place where nearly everyone, regardless of race, would want to dine.

In actuality, however, Hooper's was a restaurant rather renowned for its "whites only" policies. There were a number of restaurants in Baltimore where Negroes could be served, but Hooper's, in 1960, was a place locally famous for not serving Negroes. Thus, the wave of sit-in demonstrations which were being held in segregated facilities in Baltimore at that time tended to center on Hooper's.

When the sit-in demonstrators entered the revolving door, they were met by the hostess, who, on order of Hooper, told them that "solely on the basis of their color" they would not be served and asked them to leave the premises. The demonstrators did not go.

Instead, they went to tables, took seats and refused to leave, insisting that they be served.

On orders of Hooper, police were called, but they refused to arrest the Negroes until a warrant had been obtained. With that, Hooper went to the police station and obtained a warrant for the arrest of the Negroes, who were duly taken into custody by police. They were convicted under Maryland's trespass law. The convictions were upheld by the Maryland Court of Appeals, and the issue went to the Supreme Court as *Bell v. Maryland.* It was argued October 14 and 15, 1963, and decided June 22, 1964.

Bell v. Maryland (378 U.S. 226) was one of several sit-in cases which were decided at the same time. Each was interesting, and each questioned the authority of the state to enforce private discrimination. In one of the cases, *Robinson v. Florida,* the outcome hinged on the fact that there was a state and city law "requiring separate toilet and lavatory rooms" for Negroes in restaurants. Justice Black, for a unanimous Court, said, "While these Florida regulations do not directly and expressly forbid restaurants to serve both white and colored people together, they certainly embody a state policy putting burdens upon any restaurant which serves both races; burdens bound to discourage the serving of the two races together." The Court found "state action" to enforce racial discrimination and declared it illegal.

That was the only case where the Justices were unanimous. In the other four cases, including *Bell v. Maryland,* the nine Justices were sharply divided. Justices Douglas and Goldberg felt one way, but for different reasons. Justices Black, Harlan and White were in agreement on views sharply opposed to those of Justice Douglas. Chief Justice Warren agreed with Justice Goldberg on some points and with Justices Brennan, Clark and Stewart on others. Not only were the disagreements pronounced, but the language used by the Justices in denouncing one another's views was colorful and astringent.

The result was total disappointment. Unable to agree on the important constitutional questions, the Justices reversed the convictions of the sit-in demonstrators in all four cases on extremely narrow, legal, technical grounds. In two cases from South Carolina, they maintained the law was so written as to make entering a premises trespassing, but remaining there after being told to leave not trespassing, a strained construction which caused Justice Black to say the demonstrators would laugh at it, for they knew they were breaking the law.

The fourth case was *Griffin v. Maryland,* which had twice been argued before the Court. In this case a group of Negroes had entered Glen Echo Amusement Park in Montgomery County, Maryland, which is in the Washington, D.C., suburbs. They were arrested by a private detective named Francis J. Collins, who was hired by the owners of the park to keep Negroes out by enforcing the trespass law. The case was ultimately decided on the grounds that Collins was a deputy sheriff in addition to being a private detective and wore the badge on his uniform. This was held to be state action—that is, an arrest by a deputy sheriff—a ruling which three Justices considered most farfetched.

Even these tenuous arguments were unavailable in *Bell v. Maryland.* Police had not made the arrest and, in fact, had refused to arrest the demonstrators until Hooper had sworn out a warrant. This is akin to a homeowner who, having asked trespassers to leave his property, then swears out a warrant which police are duty-bound to serve regardless of whether they approve or disapprove of the homeowner or his warrant. The law in Maryland was properly written, so it could not be misunderstood. It seemed to be a perfect confrontation of civil and property rights, an excellent means to decide whether a private citizen could call the police to enforce his personal prejudices.

The Court ducked the issue. It noted that between the time of the arrest of the Negroes in Hooper's restaurant and the case reaching the Supreme Court, the state of Maryland had passed a law outlawing racial discrimination in places of public accommodation. It was only fair, said the Court, to send the matter back to the state courts for decision in light of the new law. This decision pleased absolutely no one and solved none of the issues.

Justice Douglas gave a stinging rebuke to his colleagues for their indecision—and a ringing advocacy of the cause of judicial activism —in these words:

"The whole nation has to face the issue; Congress is consistently counseling it; some municipalities have had to make it their first order of concern; law enforcement officers are deeply implicated, North as well as South; the question is at the root of demonstrations, unrest, riots and violence in various areas. The issue in other words commands the public attention. Yet we stand mute, avoiding the decision of the issue by an obvious pretense. . . .

"We have in this case a question that is basic to our way of life and fundamental in our constitutional scheme. No question preoccupies the country more than this one; it is plainly justiciable; it presses for a decision one way or another; we should resolve it. The people should know that when filibusters occupy other forums, when oppressions are great, when the clash of authority between the individual and the state is severe, they can still get justice in the courts. When we default, as we do today, the prestige of the law in the life of the nation is weakened."

Professor Paulsen of Columbia has called Justice Douglas' views exaggerated. He has said that even if the Court had reached a decision, it would not have solved the racial problems of employment, housing, poor education, poverty. Nor would the solution to the sit-in problem affect the businessman who discourages Negro customers by poor service, shoddy merchandise, calculated insult.

Justice Douglas made it clear that he feels that in the area of public accommodations, at least, that when a merchant caters to the public, the public's rights take precedence over the proprietor's private rights. A man's right to eat in a restaurant is part of his right to travel. It is part of his citizenship to eat and sleep in a public place, in Justice Douglas' view.

Justice Goldberg, in his long opinion, maintained that the right to free access to public accommodations was intended by the framers of the Fourteenth Amendment.

Justice Black was most outspoken on the side of the businessman: "We can only say that the Fourteenth Amendment does not of itself—of itself—contain any police regulation telling business and professional men how to conduct their affairs." He noted that a statute could draw a more precise line than a court decision could. He said the legislature could create an exception—for one type of business, etc.,—"but a constitutional rule applies to the smallest business as to the largest, to the most personal professional relationship as to the most impersonal. . . .

"This Court has never said in the school segregation decision or any before or since that the prejudice of private individuals could be laid to the state. . . . This Court has done much in carrying out its solemn duty to protect people from unlawful discriminations, and it will, of course, continue to carry out this duty as it has in the past. But the Fourteenth Amendment, of itself, does not compel either a black man or a white man running his own private business to trade with anyone else against his will. . . . We do not believe the Fourteenth Amendment was written or designed to interfere with a storekeeper's right to choose his customers or with a property owner's right to choose his social or business association, so long as he does not break federal or state laws."

Justice Black continued, "It would betray our whole plan for a tranquil and orderly society to say that a citizen, because of his personal prejudice, habits, attitudes and beliefs, is cast outside the law's protection and cannot call for the aid of officers sworn to uphold the law. The worst citizen, no less than the best, is entitled to equal protection of the laws of his state and his nation. None of our past cases justifies reading the Fourteenth Amendment in a way that might penalize citizens who are law-abiding enough to call upon the law and courts for protection instead of using their own physical strength or . . . weapons to preserve their rights."

Justice Black spoke most pointedly to those who would use violence to obtain civil rights. "The Constitution does not confer upon any group the right to substitute rule by force for rule by law. Force leads to violence, violence to mob rule by the strongest group with control of the most deadly weapons. At times the rule of law seems too slow to rely upon for the settlement of grievances, but it is the plan our nation has chosen to preserve both liberty and equality for all."

It would be unwise for even the greatest admirer of Justice Black's literary style and eloquence and his historic and unparalleled defense of individual liberties to predict that his view will prevail when the question of civil versus property rights is finally settled.

And it is likely that it will be settled, perhaps by the time you read this. Twelve days after the Court's indecision in *Bell v. Maryland,* President Johnson signed the Civil Rights Act of 1964 into law, prohibiting discrimination against Negroes in places of public accommodation. Cases challenging the constitutionality of the statute are before the Court.

If the high bench holds the law constitutional, as it seems likely to do, it will spend the next several years deciding the related issues: What is a public accommodation? Are a shoe store and a barbershop public accommodations? What is discrimination? Is an insult, poor service, rudeness discrimination? If "civil-rights demonstrators" enter a restaurant and just sit around taking up space, can a proprietor evict them?

The problems involved in the gray area between private and public discrimination are great and likely to occupy headlines for the rest of this century. What is a private club and when is it a ruse to avoid racial integration? Can a veterans or fraternal organization "blackball" a Negro on the basis of race? If a political organization meets in a person's home, can he refuse admission to a Negro member? Can a church refuse membership to a person on account of race? The application of these conflicts to housing, employment, medicine provides much fuel for legal controversy.

A key to all these matters lies in the question: What is state action? Is it state action to enforce discrimination when a policeman serves a warrant as the officers did in *Bell v. Maryland?* Is it state action when a liquor license, zoning permit or similar certificate is granted to an establishment that discriminates against Negroes? Is the state endorsing discrimination when it inspects the sanitation conditions or elevators or puts out the fire in a building whose owners refuse to rent to Negroes?

In years to come the courts will be asked to decide a number of questions stemming from the voting-rights legislation passed by Congress in 1965. The Court has already made some decisions in this area. Key provisions of the Voting Rights Act of 1965 were upheld. These protect the rights of Negroes to vote in the South and of Puerto Ricans to vote in New York. Poll taxes were ruled unconstitutional as denial of equal protection of the laws under the Fourteenth Amendment. Previous interpretations of criminal statutes were greatly expanded to permit federal prosecution of individuals who use violence to deprive a person of his civil rights. Consequently seventeen men accused of killing three civil-rights workers in Neshobe County, Mississippi, and six alleged members of the Ku

Klux Klan charged with murdering a Negro educator from Washington were made eligible for federal prosecution. To be decided are constitutional questions arising from convictions or acquittals by juries from which Negroes were excluded, elections wherein Negroes were disenfranchised, and other related matters.

If one has the feeling that one would not like to be a Justice of the Supreme Court and have to decide these questions, one will find scant comfort in the knowledge that these are the easy issues. They involve the elimination of segregation or discrimination. The dominant opinion in this country seems to favor a breakdown of racial barriers. The problems so far expressed involve the accomplishment of this goal, while retaining maximum individual freedom.

The really difficult problems of the future will stem from attempts to enforce integration. Much legal discussion has been devoted to this question: Granted the Constitution forbids segregation, but does it compel integration?

Negroes quite understandably feel that they have been deprived of equal rights and equal opportunities long enough. Their cry, borne on countless placards in thousands of demonstrations, is "Freedom Now." All deliberate speed is too slow. They want equality in education, in housing, in access to public accommodations, in the paycheck, so they can buy the necessities and luxuries so long denied them. But the freedom which stems from a bulging pocketbook is not easy to come by when you have been denied equal education, comparable training, union membership for a century.

In time, given equality of education, the social, economic and cultural inequities almost surely will be eliminated as children of both races become classmates and friends and co-workers. This process may take a generation at least, perhaps two. It is a case of equality for the children of you reading this book or, perhaps, your grandchildren. We will have landed men on the moon long before a Negro joins a country club in Jackson, Mississippi, or Grosse Point, Michigan.

To speed this equalization process, prominent Negro leaders, such as Representative Adam Clayton Powell of New York, are already speaking of governmental actions to compensate the Negro for his century of denial. Under such a system the Negro would be given

preferred status in regard to jobs, college placement, training programs, housing, in order to help him to draw abreast white men who
have enjoyed unrestricted freedom.

This process is already at work in efforts to eliminate *"de facto"*
(from the Latin meaning "in fact," "in reality") segregation of
schools. In many, perhaps most, cities integration is purely nominal.
Only a few schools have substantial numbers of Negro children in
attendance with white children. Most schools are more than 90 per
cent white or 90 per cent Negro, not because of educational policies
but because of housing patterns. Negroes, particularly in Northern
cities, are heavily ghettoized, and the schools, which are attended by
children from adjacent neighborhoods, are just as racially segregated as they were before *Brown v. Board.*

In many Northern cities, notably Chicago and New York, Negro
leaders have brought pressure on school boards to abandon the
neighborhood school policy and to work out arrangements whereby
Negro children are taken on buses to white schools located out of
the ghetto and white children bused into the ghetto. Since families
tend to settle near the schools their children attend, the drive to
eliminate *de facto* segregation is a means of changing housing
patterns—or of forcing integration.

Attempts have been made to have *de facto* school segregation
declared unconstitutional, thus forcing school boards to bus children. Some courts, notably in California and New York, have so
ruled, but the leading opinion comes from Gary, Indiana, where
U.S. District Judge George Beame said, "The neighborhood school is
a long and well-established institution in American public school
education" and there is no requirement "that a school system
developed on the neighborhood school plan, honestly and conscien-
tiously constructed with no intention or purpose to segregate the
races, must be destroyed or abandoned because the resulting effect
is to have a racial imbalance in certain schools where the district is
populated almost entirely by Negroes or whites."

The Circuit Court of Appeals has upheld the opinion, and the
Supreme Court has refused to review. Such refusal does not mean
the Justices agree with the lower-court ruling. In fact, the Supreme
Court left standing New York court rulings which upheld the decision of the New York City Board of Education to merge white and

Negro school districts in the Jackson Heights section of the city. The conflicting high-court actions may mean the Justices feel the matter is for the lower courts to decide; it may mean they don't want to decide the issue at this time; or it may indicate they wish a better case on which to make a ruling. It leaves the door open for them to take an appeal at some time in the future, when they believe issues are more clearly drawn. On the other hand, there is no assurance the Court will ever take the case. At this writing, the Court has refused to review *de facto* school-segregation cases on four occasions. Nevertheless, this seems to be a legal issue likely to be fought in the future.

Negro leadership is making a concerted drive all over the country to register Negro voters in order to make better use of their considerable political power. In some cities Negroes make up to 30 to 50 per cent of the population, yet fill only a handful of elected offices.

Improving the ratio of Negroes in city councils and state legislatures, it is reasonable to assume, will bring passage of integration laws. For instance, a law could be passed compelling apartment-house owners, particularly those using public funds, to rent a certain percentage—say, 30 per cent—of their housing units to Negroes. Would this law be constitutional?

Or a law could be passed limiting the number of Negroes who can occupy a housing project or apartment house to 25 per cent of the total. The thought here is that if more than 25 per cent are Negroes, the white residents tend to move out, making the project entirely Negro. By limiting the number of Negro occupants, the whites remain and true integration of the races occurs. Would such a law be constitutional?

Suppose a law were passed specifying that for a two-year period only Negroes can be hired for certain jobs, in order to create greater employment opportunities for Negroes. Would such a law be constitutional? Suppose zoning codes were changed to specify that the maximum number of Negroes permitted to move into any one area is 35 per cent, again with the view to force integration. Would this be legal? Suppose a law were adopted granting tax exemptions to any corporation which had 20 per cent of its employees Negro or to a landlord who rented 20 per cent of his apartments to Negroes or to banks who made 10 per cent of their loans to Negroes or to stores that issued 15 per cent of their charge accounts to Negroes. Would these laws be constitutional?

Prevailing legal opinion today is that they would not. The whole tone of Supreme Court decisions, the entire effort of Thurgood Marshall and the NAACP, has been to win for the Negro in America the "equal protection of the laws"—not special favors under the law.

"The Constitution is color-blind," said Justice Harlan in his great dissent in *Plessy v. Ferguson.* Thus, how can it be used to help the Negro any more than to hurt him? "We surrender something," wrote Henry P. Monaghan, assistant professor of law at Boston University in a marvelous article in that university's law review, "if our government adopts a policy of viewing men differently because of the texture of their skin or the content of their creed. This is, is it not, in large part what gave impetus to the 'Negro Revolution' in the first place. . . ."

Most constitutional schools believe the Constitution does not permit the forcing of the races together. This is the so-called "Parker Dictum," quoted at the beginning of this chapter. That is today's view. But, as we have seen, a few new Justices, a Constitutional amendment, an act of Congress, a change in the dominant opinion of the people—and enactments to force integration are ruled constitutional.

But suppose this does not happen. Suppose the Parker Dictum remains the law of the land. Suppose Judge Beame's ruling in the Gary, Indiana, *de facto* segregation case is not upset. What happens then?

For a decade this country has seen rampant civil disobedience. The technique of "ins" has been used to pressure public officials and businessmen into changing racial policies.

We are seeing this same technique of civil disobedience, courting arrest, court tests, appeals, etc., being used—and often by the same people—to force a change in American foreign policy. These "Vietniks," as the press has labeled them, seek an end to the draft and a cessation of aerial bombing in Vietnam, contending these are immoral.

In the future the nation is likely to see increased use of peaceful civil disobedience to eliminate *de facto* segregation in education, housing and employment and many other places, programs and situations—some unimaginable today—which a trained cadre of demonstrators take into their heads as "immoral."

The techniques and philosophies of the integrationists have undergone a significant change, marked by greater militancy, interpretation of nonviolence as weakness, advocacy of "black nationalism." These ideas, usually labeled "extremist" by more moderate civil-rights groups, are embodied in the words "black power." Its advocates, usually younger Negroes, seek to have Negroes organize themselves into a bloc to achieve maximum effectiveness from their political, economic and social power. The concept of black power connotes what has been called "reverse racism" and separatism of Negroes from American society, an attitude decried by the NAACP and other groups. The result has been a serious split in civil-rights forces.

Along with these changes in philosophy have come new techniques to achieve the benefits long denied to Negroes. Rioting, looting, arson, murder, have broken out in Los Angeles, Chicago, New York, Cleveland, Rochester, N.Y., and other cities. This rioting is usually spontaneous, but sometimes it is planned or at least endorsed by Negro leaders who see it as an ultimate technique to force white citizens to correct abuses of Negro civil and economic rights. Others dread the riots, not only as morally and economically damaging to Negroes living in ghettos but also as damaging to the entire Negro cause. These persons fear the violence will cement white antipathy to the Negro goals.

No great legal issue seems to be involved in violence. Violence is clearly illegal in this country, leaving the rioters open for legal and civil prosecution. Black nationalist leaders are aware of this, but choose to take an extralegal course to achieve their ends.

There is a great pitfall in indiscriminate use of civil disobedience. It is one thing to demonstrate against an *illegal* situation but quite another to demonstrate against a *legal* one. It may be one thing to stage a demonstration against an illegally segregated park in Birmingham, Alabama, and quite another to demonstrate against the legal neighborhood school policy in Chicago. It may be one thing to be arrested while attempting to gain entry into an illegally segregated restaurant in Baltimore, Maryland, and quite another to be arrested after publicly burning a draft card—one of the means of protest being taken to the courts. It may be one thing to sit in a five-and-dime store lunch counter demanding service and quite another to sit in the middle of Washington's Pennsylvania Avenue or to throw garbage on a bridge or to chain oneself to the door of a courthouse.

All of these techniques may have the advantage of dramatizing a point of view and calling the public attention to a right or to a wrong or to a half-right or to a partly-wrong, but some of these demonstrations are illegal and punishable under the law.

Civil-rights demonstrators avoided conviction because the Southern segregation laws under which they were arrested were in themselves illegal or, in the case of trespass laws, a sympathetic Supreme Court found a loophole by which to avoid punishing them.

If demonstrators try to apply the techniques of civil disobedience to *de facto* segregation, to private discrimination and to other aspects of American life which are found to be legal, the protestors are open to fines and imprisonment. They can be sued by the injured parties. Perhaps worse, the perpetrators will have a criminal record which will bar them from government employment and many other jobs, from military service, from jury duty and other privileges of citizenship.

Civil disobedience can be an effective technique—and a dangerous one. "There is no immunity conferred by our Constitution and laws of the United States to those individuals who insist upon practicing civil disobedience under the guise of demonstrating and protesting for 'civil rights,'" wrote U.S. District Judge Frank M. Johnson in ruling that 167 demonstrators arrested in Montgomery, Alabama, must be prosecuted.

"The philosophy that a person may, if his cause is labeled 'civil rights' or 'states rights,' determine for himself what laws and court decisions are morally right or wrong and either obey or refuse to obey them according to his own determination is a philosophy that is foreign to our 'rule of law' theory of government.

"Those who resort to civil disobedience . . . cannot and should not escape arrest and prosecution. Civil disobedience by 'civil rights workers' in the form of 'going limp' and lying or marching in the streets or upon the sidewalks, or taking to the streets to do their parading and picketing in lieu of using the sidewalks, while failing to make any application to city authorities for a parade permit, is still a violation of the law and subjects the violators to being prosecuted in the courts of the cities and states where such occurs.

"Demonstrations and protests in a disorderly and unpeaceful and unlawful manner are not sanctioned by the law as this court understands it. There is a place in our system for citizens, both Negro and white, who wish to protest civil wrongs or present grievances against violations of their rights to do so, provided they act in a peaceful and orderly manner and provided they resort to the courts and not to the streets when they are thwarted in the exercise of this privilege by authorities acting under color of the law."

That great defender of minority rights and individual liberty, Justice Black, in a 1965 dissenting opinion, issued this warning:

" . . . Minority groups . . . are the ones who always have suffered and always will suffer the most when street multitudes are allowed to substitute their pressures for the less glamorous but more dependable and temperate processes of the law. . . .

"Experience demonstrates that it is not a far step from what seems the earnest, honest, patriotic, kind-spirited multitude of today, to the fanatical, threatening, lawless mob of tomorrow. And the crowds that press in the streets for noble goals today can be supplanted tomorrow by street mobs pressuring the courts for precisely opposite ends. . . .

"Those who encourage minority groups to believe that the United States Constitution and federal laws give them a right to patrol and picket the streets whenever they choose, in order to advance what they think to be a just and noble end, do no service to those minority groups, their cause, or their country."

Two recent cases have taken this line. Both were 5–4 decisions, with Justice Black acting as "swing man." In one, the Court exposed all national civil-rights organizations to civil damage suits for the illegal actions of individual members by allowing a $65,000 judgment to stand against the NAACP. The judgment was for illegal picketing of a grocery store by members of the Savannah, Georgia, chapter of the NAACP. In the second case, the Court refused to allow arrested civil-rights demonstrators to remove their cases from state to federal courts by contending that they would be denied a fair trial because of their race. The Court said such a change in procedure would have to be enacted into law by Congress.

VII. THOU SHALT NOT
PRAY IN SCHOOL

> *. . . Religion is too personal, too sacred, too holy to permit its "unhallowed perversion" by a civil magistrate . . .* —Justice Hugo L. Black for the Supreme Court in ENGLE V. VITALE

On June 26, 1962, the Supreme Court announced its decision in *Engle v. Vitale,* and thereby embroiled itself in one of the great controversies of its history. By a 6–1 majority, the Justices declared unconstitutional a twenty-two-word prayer drafted by the New York State Board of Regents and recommended for use in the public-school classrooms of that state.

The decision was no more than announced than public opinion erupted. Clergymen of all faiths who had not seen fit to comment on a Supreme Court decision in decades hurried to praise or condemn the decision. Political leaders of all persuasions left no breath undrawn to make their opinions known. The less exalted of all faiths were surprised by the Court ruling, to say the least.

The views expressed ranged from the thoughtful to the abusive. It must be assumed that a good many of those who spoke first and thought second might wish to have their comments forgotten, but all are part of the history of our times and deserve repeating.

"The recitation of prayers in the public schools," said the New York Board of Rabbis, the largest rabbinical body in the world, "which is tantamount to the teaching of prayers, is not in conformity with the spirit of the American concept of separation of church and state. All the religious groups in this country will best advance their respective faiths by adhering to this principle."

"I am shocked and frightened," Francis Cardinal Spellman of New York said, "that the Supreme Court has declared unconstitutional a simple and voluntary declaration of belief in God by public school children. The decision strikes at the very heart of the Godly tradition in which American children have so long been raised."

James Francis Cardinal McIntyre of Los Angeles said, "The decision is positively shocking and scandalizing. . . . It is not a decision according to law, but a decision of license. In denying the privilege of prayer to God, under the law, the Court is biting the hand that feeds it. This because all law comes from God. Yet the Court presumes to deny to the children of God in a school the opportunity to speak to the Creator, the Lawmaker, the Preserver of Mankind. This denial puts the shame on our faces, as we are forced to emulate Mr. Khrushchev [then the Soviet Union's Premier]."

The Reverend Arthur L. Kinsolving, president of the Protestant Council of Churches of New York, said, "Ultimately we will have to revise the decision and find some way back to the religious foundations of this country."

"In citing the unconstitutionality of prayer reading in the public schools," said the Reverend Dr. D. McLean Greeley, president of the Unitarian Universalist Association, "the Supreme Court has acted clearly in support of the principle of separation of church and state as guaranteed by the First Amendment to the Constitution."

Dean M. Kelly, director of the National Council of Churches' Department of Religious Liberty, said, "Many Christians will welcome the decision. It protects the religious rights of minorities and guards against the development of public school religion which is neither Christianity nor Judaism, but something less than either."

Dr. Sterling M. McMurrin, U.S. Commissioner of Education, said, "I believe it's no loss to religion but may be a gain in clarifying matters. Prayer that is essentially a ceremonial classroom function has not much religious value."

A. M. Sonnabend, then president of the American Jewish Committee, said, "Prayer in our democratic society is a matter for the home, synagogue and church and not for state institutions."

"There is plenty of opportunity afforded to parents to inculcate religious faith in their children at home and at weekend religious schools," said Senator Jacob Javits, New York Republican.

Representative John J. Rooney, a New York Democrat, disagreed, saying the Court decision put United States schools on a par with Russian schools.

Representative Frank J. Becker, New York Republican, called the decision "the most tragic in the history of the United States."

Representative Emanuel Celler, another New York Republican, disputed this, saying, "All parties agreed that the prayer was religious in nature. This being so, it ran counter to the First Amendment, which is well grounded in history and has saved the United States from religious strife."

Senator Herman E. Talmadge, a Georgia Democrat, said, "An outrageous edict which has numbed the conscience and shocked the highest sensibilities of the nation."

Representative John Bell Williams, a Mississippi Democrat, said the ruling was "a deliberate and completely planned conspiracy to substitute materialism for spiritual values."

Representative L. Mendel Rivers, South Carolina Democrat, said the Court "now officially states its disbelief in God Almighty" and accused the Justices of adjudicating "with one eye on the Kremlin and the other on the NAACP."

The nation's three living former Presidents were heard from. President Harry S Truman said, "The Supreme Court, of course, is the interpreter of the Constitution."

President Dwight D. Eisenhower declared, "I always thought this nation was established as a religious one."

President Herbert Hoover opined, "The Congress should at once submit an amendment to the Constitution which establishes the right to religious devotions in all government agencies, national, state and local." He called the Court ruling "a disintegration of a sacred American heritage."

The day after the decision was announced two constitutional amendments were submitted in Congress, merely the first of scores to be drafted.

President John F. Kennedy was asked about the Court opinion at his news conference a day or so after the decision was announced. He said, "We have in this case a very easy remedy and that is to pray ourselves. And I would think that it would be a welcome reminder to every American family that we can pray a good deal more at home, we can attend our church with a good deal more frequency and we can make the true meaning of prayer much more important in the training of all our children. . . . I would hope that as a result of the decision, all American parents will intensify their efforts at home, and the rest of us will support the Constitution and the responsibility of the Supreme Court in interpreting it."

There can be little doubt that many of the men who rendered opinions about the decision, whether pro or con, had not read the decision. With only a handful of exceptions, newspapers omitted a vital portion of the opinion which would have eliminated a great deal of public misunderstanding. This episode in the Court's history might be called "The Case of the Missing Footnote."

It would make a good "thriller," for the decision, rather the misunderstanding of it, periled the Court as few decisions have. As we have tried to demonstrate, the Court's power relies on "dominant opinion." The flood of mail to the Court and the torrent of public comment indicated that dominant opinion was clearly against the decision.

The problem lay in the fact that incompletely informed reporters and commentators read into the decision a great deal that it did not say. Fear quickly developed that the Court's ruling had secularized American life. Not only would prayers go out of public schools, but chaplains would be forced out of the military services, "In God We Trust" would be removed from coins, the words "under God" would be taken out of the Pledge of Allegiance, use of prayers in Congress, courts and other public meetings would be discontinued.

Worse, it seemed that all support to churches, such as tax exemptions, scholarships to students attending church colleges, income-tax deductions for church contributions, and many, many other direct and indirect governmental aids to churches would have to be eliminated.

The effect of all this, in certain sections of the public mind, was the creation of a Godless nation, abandoning and abandoned by the Deity, Who had aided us in numberless national perils in the past and was our shield in battle. Didn't "The Star-Spangled Banner," "America," "America the Beautiful," "God Bless America," the Declaration of Independence, the Constitution and most of the cherished artifacts of our nationalism refer to and enlist the support of the Supreme Being? Now the Court had tossed all that aside—or so the misinformed initially believed.

To stretch *Engle v. Vitale* to do all this was to ask a great deal of it. The case was brought by Steven I. Engle and other parents of eleven children in the New Hyde Park School District on Long Island, New York. They wanted the Board of Education, of which William J. Vitale, Jr., was a member, to stop using the New York State Regents prayer.

A more innocuous prayer there could hardly be. It said, "Almighty God, we acknowledge our dependence upon Thee, and we beg Thy blessing upon us, our parents, our teachers and our country."

The prayer had been drafted in 1951 in reply to criticism that New York State public schools were derelict in their teaching of religious and moral values. The prayer was carefully drafted to be as interdenominational as possible, offending neither Catholic, Protestant or Jew. Even Moslems, Hindus and Buddhists would find little to complain about. The prayer was recommended for use in public schools at the start of classes each day. Many school systems adopted the recommendation, including the district at New Hyde Park. Children who did not wish to participate were exempted. They could leave the room or remain silent as the teachers led the classes in the recitation of the prayer.

What was so surprising to the vast majority of Americans, regardless of their religious affiliation, was that anyone could take offense at such a prayer. It was bland, devoid of theology and calculated to offend no one.

Yet, the five parents of the eleven children did object. Two of the parents were Jewish, one was a member of the Ethical Culture Society, one was Unitarian and one was a nonbeliever. They contended the prayer conflicted with their religious beliefs. They further objected to the stigma attached to their children when they did not participate in the prayers.

Their petition challenging the constitutionality of the school prayer was rejected by the New York Court of Appeals by a 5–2 margin. When it went to the Supreme Court the vote was 6–1. Justice Felix Frankfurter was ill and did not participate. Justice Byron "Whizzer" White joined the Court after the case had been argued. Opinion for the Court was written by Justice Black, the great activist, the defender of individual liberties.

"There can be no doubt," said Justice Black, "that New York's State prayer program officially establishes the religious beliefs embodied in the prayer. . . .

"Neither the fact that the prayer may be denominationally neutral nor the fact that its observance on the part of students is voluntary can serve to free it from the limitation of the Establishment Clause, as it might from the Free Exercise Clause, of the First Amendment. . . ."

Justice Black was referring to the sixteen words in the First Amendment to the Constitution: "Congress shall make no law respecting an establishment of religion or prohibiting the free exercise thereof. . . ." These words are our national guarantee that no government shall pass a law which creates an official religion or prohibits or in any way restricts the practice of any religion.

"When the power, prestige and financial support of government is placed behind a particular religious belief," Justice Black continued, "the indirect coercive pressure upon religious minorities to conform to the prevailing officially approved religion is plain. . . .

"Its [the establishment clause's] first and most immediate purpose rested on the belief that a union of government and religion tends to destroy government and degrade religion. The history of governmentally established religions, both in England and in this country, showed that whenever government had allied itself with one particular form of religion, the inevitable result had been that it had incurred the hatred, disrespect and even contempt of those who held contrary beliefs. That same history showed that many people had lost their respect for any religion that had relied upon the support of government to spread its faith. The Establishment Clause thus stands as an expression of principle on the part of the formulators of our Constitution that religion is too personal, too sacred, too holy, to permit its 'unhallowed perversion' by a civil magistrate. . . .

"It is neither sacrilegious nor anti-religious to say that . . . government in this country should stay out of the business of writing or sanctioning official prayers and leave that plainly religious function to the people themselves or to those the people choose to look to for religious guidance."

At this point Justice Black made a notation for Footnote Number 21, which read: "There is of course nothing reached here that is inconsistent with the fact that school children and others are officially encouraged to express love for our country by reciting historical documents such as the Declaration of Independence which contain references to the Deity or by singing officially-espoused anthems which contain the composer's profession of faith in a Supreme Being or with the fact that there are many manifestations in our public life of belief in God. Such patriotic or ceremonial occasions bear no true resemblance to the unquestioned religious exercise that the State of New York sponsored in this instance."

Clearly, those critics of the opinion who expressed fears that "In God We Trust" would be taken off coins, that prayers in Congress would be disbanded, that "religion has been taken out of the schools," or that all manifestation of Godliness would be removed from American public life were unacquainted with Footnote 21.

That so many newspaper accounts of the Court's opinion failed to mention this vital footnote led to a change in the Supreme Court's practices. Previously all decisions were announced on Monday. Sometimes there would be a score or more of important opinions, making it a superhuman task for reporters accurately to report their contents. Now the Court announces its decisions when they are reached.

Justice Douglas wrote a concurring opinion. The dissenting opinion was by Justice Potter Stewart, an Ohioan, graduate of Yale Law School, who had known both the law offices of New York's Park Avenue and the legal practices of Cincinnati. He was named first to the Court of Appeals and then to the Supreme Court by President Eisenhower.

"With all respect," wrote Justice Stewart, "I think the Court has misapplied a great constitutional principle. I cannot see how an official religion is established by letting those who want to say a prayer say it. On the contrary, I think that to deny the wish of those school children to join in reciting the prayer is to deny them their opportunity of sharing in the spiritual heritage of our nation. . . .

"We deal here not with the establishment of a state church, which would, of course, be constitutionally impermissible, but with whether school children who want to begin their day by joining in prayer must be prohibited from doing so."

Justice Stewart made note of the reference to God in the Pledge of Allegiance and the "Star-Spangled Banner," the statements of many Presidents importuning God's help, the Act of Congress asking the President to proclaim a National Day of Prayer and the motto on coins.

"Countless similar examples could be listed," Justice Stewart said, "but there is no need to belabor the obvious. It was all summed up by this court 10 years ago in a single sentence: 'We are a religious people whose ancestors presupposed a Supreme Being. . . .'

"I do not believe that this court or the Congress or the President has, by their actions and practices I have mentioned, established an 'official religion' in violation of the Constitution, and I do not believe the State of New York has done so in this case. What each has done has been to recognize and to follow the deeply entrenched and highly cherished spiritual tradition of our nation. . . ."

Justice Stewart expressed in eloquence that which the majority of Americans believe—that we are a Godly nation. Yet there is a fallacy to his reasoning which even nonlegal observers were quick to spot. It is that no one has to be President, a Supreme Court Justice, a member of Congress, but every American child under age sixteen must attend school. It is the child's lack of free choice in the matter, the coercion of the law upon him, that the other six Justices felt put the question beyond the reach of eloquence.

All *Engle v. Vitale* did—observers contended—was to hold that a prayer prescribed by an official governmental agency, such as the New York State Board of Regents, was unconstitutional because it led to the establishment of an official religion. Footnote 21 and other portions of the Court's opinion made it clear that the Court was not, at this time certainly, saying anything which had any effect on other manifestations of religiousness in national life.

While technically true, this statement concerning *Engle v. Vitale* was an oversimplification. Most Court observers knew that all religious exercises in schools, not just the New York prayer, were doomed.

The end came a year later when the Court announced its decision in *School District of Abington Township, Pennsylvania v. Schempp* and *Murray v. Curlett*. By an 8–1 margin the Court declared that recitation of the Lord's Prayer and the reading of passages from the Holy Bible in schools were unconstitutional.

The Pennsylvania case was brought by Edward Lewis Schempp and his wife, Sidney, on behalf of their children, Roger and Donna, who attended the Abington Township Schools near Philadelphia. The Schempps were Unitarian and they objected to the religious exercises in school.

The exercises were broadcast into the classroom prior to the start of the day's classes by members of the school's radio and television workshop. Over the school intercom a student would read ten or more verses of the Bible which he had chosen, then recite the Lord's Prayer, during which time the teacher in each classroom and the students would join in repeating the prayer. Following that, there would be the flag salute and recitation of the Pledge of Allegiance, then announcements by the school principal.

All of this was pursuant to a Pennsylvania law which reads: "At least 10 verses from the Holy Bible shall be read, without comment, at the opening of each public school in each school day. Any child shall be excused from such Bible readings or attending such Bible readings upon the written request of his parents or guardian."

Schempp did not ask for his children to be excused for fear they would be "labeled as odd balls." He knew, he said, that children and teachers tend to think of all persons with different religious beliefs as "atheists," which has an "un-American" connotation to it. Too, Schempp felt that for his children to stand outside in the hallway resembled punishment for bad conduct. Besides, they'd miss the announcements which were important to the children.

The second case was brought by Mrs. Madalyn Murray of Baltimore on behalf of her son, William J. Murray III. Mrs. Murray said she was an atheist and intended to raise her son as an atheist. Years later Mrs. Murray admitted to the author during interviews that it was her son, a junior-high-school student at the time, who propelled her into bringing the suit. She would have dropped it except that he felt as a matter of principle he should not participate in the prayers if he did not believe in them—nor would she force him to.

Mrs. Murray first tried to have her son leave the room, but the Baltimore School Superintendent ruled that he had to sit in his seat during the Lord's Prayer and Bible reading. Mrs. Murray took her son out of the school and the Board of Education later changed the ruling to allow William to leave the classroom. But by this time Mrs. Murray had filed her suit challenging the constitutionality of the religious exercises.

Both cases came together before the Court. Mindful of the furor that had greeted *Engel v. Vitale*, the Court set out to mold dominant opinion in support of its beliefs. Of the eight Justices who agreed, four wrote concurring opinions. Justice Tom C. Clark, a Texan and a Presbyterian, delivered the Court's opinion. Justice Douglas wrote a concurring opinion. Justice William Brennan, the Court's only Roman Catholic, wrote a long opinion, and Justice Arthur Goldberg, the Court's only Jew, wrote the fourth opinion.

Justices Clark, Brennan and Goldberg sought to lessen public fears of national Godlessness, while making it clear that religious exercises in public schools were unconstitutional.

"The place of religion in our society is an exalted one," said Justice Clark, "achieved through a long tradition of reliance on home, the church, and the invisible citadel of the individual heart and mind. We have come to recognize through bitter experience that it is not within the power of government to invade that citadel whether its purpose or effect be to aid or oppose, to advance or retard.

"In the relationship between man and religion, the state is firmly committed to a position of neutrality."

Justice Clark said that the decision had no effect on the use of the Bible to study religion or history or literature in schools.

Justice Brennan said, "The Court mandate expresses a deliberate and considered judgment that such matters are to be left to the conscience of the citizen. . . ."

Most of Justice Brennan's lengthy opinion was an effort to lessen public fears about future opinions of the Court striking down tax exemptions to churches, grants to church colleges and hospitals, use of chaplains in military service, and many other areas where the secular and sacred overlap in our society. He stated as his opinion—it has no legal standing because these were not the issues before the Court—that such governmental aids to religion are constitutional and gave his reasons why he believed so.

Justice Goldberg quoted the famous footnote from Justice Black's opinion in *Engle v. Vitale*.

Justice Stewart again dissented, but not nearly so strongly as in the earlier case. He said the matter hinged on whether children are compelled to attend the religious exercises. He suggested that the case be sent back to the lower courts for more study on this issue.

For the most part, the decision of June 1963 was greeted with far less public uproar than the ruling of a year earlier. Dominant opinion had swung around to the realization that religious freedom was freedom to all minorities, that recitation of the Lord's Prayer would be an obvious affront to all Jewish children if no one else, that our country had been founded by religious minorities, and that religion is best reserved for home, heart and church—although many there are who will disagree with that statement.

The real importance of the school-prayer cases is not in their immediate effect on education or religion but in their meaning for the future. These cases are part of a pattern of Supreme Court decisions which must extend far beyond the present. The possible direction of these decisions lies in the concurring opinions of Justice Douglas, views which if made into law could have the greatest influence on religious life in America. These will be the issues of the future.

VIII. ONE NATION UNDER GOD?

> *The First Amendment has erected a wall between church and state. That wall must be kept high and impregnable. We could not approve the slightest breach.*—Justice Hugo L. Black for the Court in EVERSON V. BOARD OF EDUCATION

The unanswered question concerning the school-prayer cases is whether they are a new direction in the Court's attitude toward religion in American life or simply a return to an old course.

If all the Justices did was to protect the rights of minorities, that is far from startling. Our nation was founded by religious minorities. Pilgrims, Puritans, English Catholics, French Huguenots and many others came to the shores of the New World to obtain free exercise of their religion.

Often the right to free exercise of religion has meant the right to private discriminations and religious prejudice. In the past far more than in these ecumenical days, religious sects were able to have and to boast their rivalries and disagreements with other sects.

Yet there have been precious few instances of official, governmental prejudices. The United States has been able to compile an amazing record for official religious tolerance. Jews, while victims of private discrimination, have found less violence, less oppression than in any other place they have ever lived, except modern Israel. The Roman Catholic Church has flourished in the New World to an extent undreamed of even in the days of the Holy Roman Empire.

The major Protestant sects—Episcopal, Methodist, Baptist, Lutheran, Presbyterian, Congregational and others—have all had the respect of the nation.

Americans have been able to embrace, with only minimal friction, witch burners, snake worshipers, Amish, Mennonites, and others who value anachronism, Shakers, "holy rollers," a wide variety of Pentecostal and fundamentalist sects, Christian Scientists, Jehovah's Witnesses, Ethical Culturists, Unitarians and Universalists, Mormons, Seventh-Day Adventists, and believers in the Church of God, the True Church of God and the Only True Church of God. We have been able as well to abide the irreligious and the nonbelievers.

Certainly religion in America has been all-embracing. We have made a specialty of religious divisiveness, and yet, as the public reaction to the school-prayer cases demonstrated, we have an assumption that we are a Godly nation and view a threat to all religion as a threat to each religion.

A major factor in our fine record of governmental religious toleration has been the "establishment" and "free exercise" clauses of the First Amendment. The language clearly said "Congress shall pass no law . . ." and that is basically what Congress did—nothing. The question of religious freedom seldom came to the courts. During the first 140 years of its existence, the Supreme Court scarcely knew that religion could be a legal question.

The first important cases involving religion to come before the Supreme Court involved the Jehovah's Witnesses, which the Court described this way: "The Witnesses are an unincorporated body teaching that the obligation imposed by law of God is superior to that of laws enacted by temporal government. Their religious beliefs include a literal version of Exodus, Chapter 20, Verses 4 and 5, which say: 'Thou shalt not make unto thee any graven image, or any likeness of anything that is in heaven above, or that is in the earth beneath, or that is in the water under the earth; thou shalt not bow down thyself to them nor serve them.' They consider that the flag is an 'image' within this command. For this reason they refuse to salute it."

One afternoon in 1946 Lillian Gobitis, aged twelve, and her brother William, ten, came home from school in the small town of

Minersville, Pennsylvania, and announced that the principal had said they were not to return to school until they agreed to salute the flag as their classmates did.

The requirement that pupils daily salute the flag and recite the Pledge of Allegiance was adopted by the Minersville Board of Education, not out of any desire to oppress the Witnesses but to promote patriotism and good citizenship. Our flag, perhaps more than other countries', is a particularly cherished symbol of national unity.

Walter Gobitis (pronounced *Go-bite-is*), the father of Lillian and William, explained over and over that he and his family and other Jehovah's Witnesses meant no disrespect to the flag. They loved their country and were as patriotic as the next person, but their religious beliefs simply forbade the worship of graven images—such as the flag. Furthermore, Gobitis didn't want the ceremony abandoned. He just wanted his children excused from the flag salute.

The school board refused and ordered the Gobitis children expelled from school, which meant under the compulsory education laws that Gobitis had to pay to send his children to private school. With the help of the American Civil Liberties Union, Gobitis went to court to compel the reinstatement of his children—without their being required to salute the flag.

The Federal District Court upheld the Gobitis view, and this opinion was upheld by the Third Circuit Court of Appeals at Philadelphia. Then the case went to the Supreme Court as *Minersville School District v. Gobitis* (310 U.S. 586). The case was argued April 25, 1940, before a Court that included Chief Justice Charles Evans Hughes, Justice Harlan F. Stone of New York, Justice James Clark McReynolds of Tennessee, Justice Owen J. Roberts of Pennsylvania and five men who were named by President Franklin Roosevelt— Justices Black, Frankfurter, Douglas, Reed and Frank Murphy of Michigan.

The case attracted unusual interest. World War II had begun in Europe. More than Jehovah's Witnesses against a school board, the case symbolized, in many minds, liberty against oppression; it symbolized to others a challenge to patriotism in a time of potential danger to the United States. The American Bar Association took great interest in the case and submitted briefs as friends of the

Court. The briefs were prepared by Grenville Clark of New York and Zechariah Chaffee, Jr., professor of law at Harvard. They were signed by those eminent attorneys in the country who supported the Gobitis family.

By a vote of 8–1, the Court decided against the Gobitis family. The Court's opinion was written by Justice Frankfurter, a Jew, an Austrian by birth, who called the case a "tragic issue" and a "clash of rights, not a clash of wrong." He wrote, "The ultimate foundation of a free society is the binding tie of cohesive sentiment." He said the flag is "the symbol of our national unity . . . the emblem of freedom in its truest, best sense. As such, the right of society to teach patriotism and national unity to a child takes precedence over the parent's religious teachings."

Justice Frankfurter almost certainly had difficulty writing the decision, particularly when he learned that Justice Stone, the great liberal and idol of Frankfurter, was to dissent. Justice Stone said that government may "make war and raise armies" but "it is a long step and one I am unable to take to the position that government may, as a supposed educational measure and as a means of disciplining the young, compel public affirmations which violate their religious conscience." He continued that it is one thing to "elicit" expressions of loyalty, another to "command" them.

The Frankfurter opinion was widely condemned, particularly in newspaper editorials, for violating America's cherished principles of individual freedom and for "surrendering to popular hysteria." At the same time, it was praised by ardent patriotic groups. Much of the legal profession was shocked at the opinion and astounded that Justice Frankfurter, the great liberal and former dean of the Harvard Law School, had written it.

Within a matter of months the Court's 8–1 majority in *Gobitis* shrank. Justice McReynolds retired and was succeeded by James F. Byrnes of South Carolina. Chief Justice Hughes retired and Justice Stone was elevated to Chief Justice. Robert H. Jackson of New York was then appointed to the bench.

Another Jehovah's Witness case came to the Court, this one involving constitutionality of municipal ordinances which required Witnesses to buy a license before selling their religious publications on street corners or from door to door. In *Jones v. Opelika* (316 U.S.

584), as this issue was called, the Court upheld the legality of the laws, but by a 5–4 majority. Joining Chief Justice Stone in the dissent were Justices Black, Douglas and Murphy, who had each voted with the majority in Gobitis. They now said, "Since we joined the opinion in the *Gobitis* case, we think this is an appropriate occasion to state that we now believe that it was also wrongly decided. Certainly our democratic form of government functioning under the historic Bill of Rights has a high responsibility to accommodate itself to the religious views of minorities, however unpopular and unorthodox those views may be."

One of the results of the Gobitis decision was that the state of West Virginia amended its laws to require compulsory flag salutes in schools. Jehovah's Witnesses Walter Barnette, Paul Stull and Lucy McClure sued in Federal District Court to stop enforcement of the act.

The high drama which was unfolding in these flag-salute cases took a strange twist when a special three-judge panel was set up at the district court to hear the case. One of the three was Judge John J. Parker of North Carolina (author of the Parker Dictum), whom President Herbert Hoover had appointed to the Supreme Court in 1930. The Senate had refused to confirm Judge Parker, in part because it was generally believed he was too likely to conform to precedent.

Judge Parker and his colleagues now threw precedent to the winds and ruled against the high court's decision in the *Gobitis* case. The issue went to the Supreme Court in 1943 as *West Virginia State Board of Education v. Barnette* (319 U.S. 624). It was clearly a rematch of *Gobitis*—and a reversal. Chief Justice Stone was joined by Justices Black, Douglas, Murphy, Jackson and Wiley Rutledge for a 6–3 majority.

The opinion by Justice Jackson is a distinctive moment in Court history. He wrote: "A person gets from a symbol the meaning he puts into it, and what is one man's comfort and inspiration is another man's jest and scorn. . . . To sustain the compulsory flag salute, we are required to say that a Bill of Rights which guards the individual's right to speak his mind left it open to public authorities to compel him to utter what is not in his mind. . . .

"Those who begin coercive elimination of dissent soon find themselves exterminating dissenters. Compulsory unification of opinion achieves only the unanimity of the graveyard. . . . It seems trite but necessary to say that the First Amendment was designed to avoid these ends by avoiding these beginnings."

Justice Jackson then wrote what is considered by some to be one of the jewels of legal prose: "If there is any fixed star in our constitutional constellation, it is that no official, high or petty, can prescribe what shall be orthodox in politics, nationalism, religion or other matters of opinion or force citizens to confess by word or act their faith therein. If there are any circumstances which permit an exception, they do not now occur to us."

Now in dissent, only three years after his majority opinion, Justice Frankfurter wrote most poignantly:

"One who belongs to the most vilified and persecuted minority in history is not likely to be insensible to the freedoms guaranteed by our Constitution. Were my purely personal attitude relevant, I should wholeheartedly associate myself with the general libertarian views in the Court's opinion, representing as they do the thought and action of a lifetime. But as judges we are neither Jew nor Gentile, neither Catholic nor agnostic. We owe equal attachment to the Constitution and are equally bound by our judicial obligations whether we derive our citizenship from the earliest or the latest immigrants to these shores.

"As a member of this Court, I am not justified in writing my private notions of policy into the Constitution, no matter how deeply I may cherish them or how mischievous I may deem their disregard."

After this excellent statement of judicial restraint, Justice Frankfurter said, "In the light of all the circumstances . . . it would require more daring than I possess to deny that reasonable legislators could have taken the action which is before us for review. The constitutional protection of religious freedom terminated disabilities, it did not create new privileges. It gave religious equality, not civil immunity. Law is concerned with external behavior and not with the inner life of man. . . . One may have the right to practice one's religion and at the same time owe the duty of formal obedience to laws that run counter to one's beliefs."

A frequent criticism of the Supreme Court is that in the school-prayer decision it moved from protection of the freedom of minority religious groups to allowing minority rule. It is one thing, the critics say, to require schools to allow Jehovah's Witnesses not to salute a flag and quite another to make the majority give up flag-saluting because Jehovah's Witnesses object to it. Of course, the Court has not done this, yet it has made the majority give up prayer and Bible recitations in schools because a minority objected.

To find in Court opinions on religious questions since *West Virginia v. Barnette* a pattern of enforcing minority rule takes a lot of looking. The men in the Marble Palace have been inconsistent and have stood on both sides of the same issue—almost at the same time.

Let's look at these principal cases, for they are the fuel that will be used to light legal fires over religion in years to come. A more difficult series of issues is hard to imagine.

Consider first the New Jersey school-bus case, *Everson v. Board of Education,* which the Court decided in 1947. The issue was this: The Board of Education of Ewing Township voted to pay the fares of children going to school on the regular buses operated by the local transportation company. Payment was also made to parents of children attending Catholic schools, which was duly challenged in the Courts.

Justice Black wrote the opinion for a divided Court, holding 5-4 that the reimbursement was legal. But Justice Black made it clear his decision was not an easy one: "The 'establishment of religion' clause of the First Amendment meant at least this: Neither a state nor the Federal Government can set up a church. Neither can pass laws which aid one religion, aid all religions, or prefer one religion over another. . . . No tax in any amount, large or small, can be levied to support any religious activities or institutions, whatever they may be called, or whatever form they may adopt to teach or practice religion."

While admitting that New Jersey could not contribute tax funds to support a religion, he said, "On the other hand, other language of the Amendment commands that New Jersey cannot hamper its citizens in the free exercise of their own religion. Consequently, it cannot exclude individual Catholics, Lutherans, Mohamedans, Baptists, Jews, Methodists, Non-believers, Presbyterians, or members of any faith, *because of their faith, or lack of it* [Justice Black's italics], from receiving the benefits of public welfare legislation."

Justice Black then turned his attention to whether providing police and fire protection, sewage and water and other similar services to churches was establishment of religion. "Of course," he said, "cutting off church schools from these services, so separate and so indisputably marked off from the religious function, would make it far more difficult for the schools to operate. But such is obviously not the purpose of the First Amendment. That Amendment requires the state to be as neutral in its relations with groups of religious believers and non-believers; it does not require the state to be their adversary. State power is no more to be used so as to handicap religions than it is to favor them. . . . The First Amendment has erected a wall between church and state. That wall must be kept high and impregnable. We could not approve the slightest breach. New Jersey has not breached it here."

In his dissent, Justice Jackson tackled the same question as Justice Black, but with an opposite result. "A policeman protects a Catholic, of course—but not because he is a Catholic; it is because he is a man and a member of our society. The fireman protects the Church school—but not because it is a Church school; it is because it is property, part of the assets of our society. . . . But before these school authorities draw a check to reimburse for a student's fare they must ask just that question, and if the school is a Catholic one they may render aid because it is such, while if it is of any other faith or is run for profit, the help must be withheld."

There was another dissenting opinion by Justice Rutledge, who asked, "Does New Jersey's action furnish support for religion by use of the taxing power? Certainly it does, if the test remains undiluted as Jefferson and Madison made it, that money taken by taxation from one is not to be used or given to support another's religious training or belief, or indeed one's own." Justice Rutledge held that the cost of transporation was part of the cost of education and religious training in Catholic schools, and therefore illegal.

The distinctions being made in *Everson* seemed clear to few—and they were to get worse. In 1948 the Court received a case, brought by Mrs. Vashti McCollum, wife of a University of Illinois professor, objecting to the released-time program in Champagne, Illinois, public schools. Released time was the practice by which clergymen held religious services in school buildings for children who wished to attend. Those who did not continued their regular secular work.

Justice Black again rendered the majority opinion, this time 8–1, in *McCollum v. Board of Education* (333 U.S. 203). Released-time religious services in public schools were held to be a violation of the First Amendment. "This is beyond all question a utilization of the tax-established and tax-supported public school system to aid religious groups and to spread their faith. And it falls squarely under the ban of the First Amendment as we interpreted it in *Everson v. Board of Education.* . . ."

Said Justice Black: "Neither a state nor the Federal government can set up a church. Neither can pass laws which aid one religion, aid all religions or prefer one religion over another."

The effect of the opinion was to eliminate the majority's desire (in Champagne, Illinois, at least) to hold released-time religious classes in public schools because a minority objected.

Four years later, in 1952, the question of dismissed-time religious classes came before the Court. Dismissed time was different from released time in that the classes were held outside the school buildings. Children who wished to go to the religious classes in churches did so. Others remained in regular classes. The case was from New York and labeled *Zorach v. Clauson* (343 U.S. 306).

The majority opinion, by Justice Douglas, upheld the legality of dismissed-time instruction. He maintained there was a difference from released time in that public funds were not used in dismissed-time classes, and he found no coercion of students to attend the religious instruction. Justice Douglas then said:

"The First Amendment within the scope of its coverage permits no exception; the prohibition [of establishment of religion] is absolute. The First Amendment, however, does not say that in every and all respects there shall be a separation of church and state. . . . That is the common sense of the matter. Otherwise, the state and religion would be aliens to each other—hostile, suspicious and even unfriendly."

Justice Douglas then said total separation would mean no police or fire protection for churches, no prayer in legislative halls, no Thanksgiving Day, etc. "We are a religious people," said Justice

Douglas, "whose institutions presuppose a Supreme Being. . . ." It was this sentence that Justice Stewart threw back at Justice Douglas in his dissent in the school-prayer cases.

A few more words from Justice Douglas' opinion will be illuminating: "When the state encourages religious instruction or cooperates with religious authorities by adjusting the schedule of public events to sectarian needs, it follows the best of our traditions. For it then respects the religious nature of our people and accommodates the public service to their spirtual needs. To hold that it may not would be to find in the Constitution a requirement that the government show a callous indifference to religious groups. That would be preferring those who believe in no religion over those who do believe. . . . But we find no constitutional requirement which makes it necessary for government to be hostile to religion and to throw its weight against efforts to widen the effective scope of religious influence."

Justice Black dissented, saying he could see little difference between released time and dismissed time and reaffirming his stand in *Everson.*

Justice Frankfurter also dissented, saying, "The day this country ceases to be free for irreligion it will cease to be free for religion— except for the sect that can win political power. . . . We start down a rough road when we begin to mix compulsory public education with compulsory Godliness."

The only other major case affecting religion prior to the school-prayer cases was in 1960 when Chief Justice Warren rendered a majority opinion that Sunday blue laws were constitutional. Sunday blue laws are so-called severe or puritanical laws which derive from a code said to have been adopted in the New England colonies. There is a welter of state and local laws on the subject; for example, in some communities certain businesses may remain open, others must close. Chief Justice Warren argued that their meaning was no longer primarily religious. ". . . the state's purpose," he said, "was not merely to provide a one-day-in-seven work stoppage. In addition to this, the state seeks to set one day apart from all others as a day of rest, repose, recreation and tranquility—a day which all members of the family and community have the opportunity to spend and enjoy together. . . ." (*McGowan v. Maryland,* 362 U.S. 959). Major problems of personal conscience arise, however, from the *McGowan v. Maryland* decision. Religious Jews are forced to close their businesses for two days—their own Sabbath, which falls on Saturday, and the Christian Sabbath, which falls on Sunday. Agnostics and atheists are forced to close in order to honor a conviction they do not believe; for according to the decision, the one-day-in-seven-day-of-rest *has* to be Sunday.

The Supreme Court's record is far from clear. It has held that religious instruction in schools is illegal but religious instruction on school time outside of schools is legal. Sunday blue laws are legal because they are not religious laws. Justice Black has held staunchly for a wall of separation between church and state, then said that paying the cost of transportation to Catholic schools does not breach the wall, a position Justice Jackson "roasted" in these words: "The case which irresistibly comes to mind as the most fitting precedent is that of Julia who, according to Byron's reports, 'whispering "I will ne'er consent"—consented.'"

The strangest of all is Justice Douglas, who, in *Zorach v. Clauson,* was a staunch defender of our religious heritage, yet in the school-prayer cases took the most extreme view of the entire Court. Compare his temperate view in the 1952 case with those expressed in his concurring opinion in *Engle v. Vitale* in 1962: "The point for decision is whether the Government can constitutionally finance a religious exercise. Our system at the Federal and state level is presently honeycombed with such financing. Nevertheless, I think it is an unconstitutional undertaking whatever form it takes."

He listed in a footnote such forms of financing as chaplains in the military service; chapel services at the military academies; religious services in federal hospitals and prisons; Presidential religious proclamations; use of Bibles in oath-taking; veterans receiving GI Bill money to attend denominational schools; World War II grants to religious schools for the training of nurses; school-lunch money to parochial schools; monies made available to nonpublic hospitals; the motto on coins; religious instruction in the National Training School for Boys; income-tax deductions for church contributions; exemption of religious organizations from income taxes.

Justice Douglas continued: "What New York does on the opening of its public schools is what we do when we open court. Our Crier has from the beginning announced the convening of the Court and then added 'God save the United States and this honorable court.' That utterance is a supplication, a prayer in which we, the judges, are free to join, but which we need not recite any more than the students need recite the New York prayer. . . ."

Justice Douglas said he could see no difference between the New York school prayer and the recitation in the Supreme Court or Congress. "No matter how briefly the prayer is said . . . the person praying is a public officer on the public payroll, performing a religious exercise in a government institution. It is said that the element of coercion is inherent in the giving of this [school] prayer. If that is true here, it is also true of the prayer with which this court is convened and of that opening the Congress. Few adults, let alone children, would leave our courtroom or the Senate or the House while their prayer is being given. Every such audience is in a sense a 'captive' audience."

Again in *Abington Township v. Schempp,* Douglas repeated this theme: "It [the establishment clause] forbids the state to employ its facilities or funds in a way that gives any church or all churches greater strength in our society than it would have by relying on its members alone. Thus, the present requirement must fall under that clause for the additional reason that public funds, though small in amount, are being used to promote religious exercises. Through the mechanism of the state, all of the people are being required to finance a religious exercise that only some of the people want and that violates the sensibilities of others.

"The most effective way to establish an institution is to finance it; and this truth is reflected in the appeals by church groups for public funds to finance their religious schools [Justice Douglas' italics]. Financing a church either in its strictly religious activities or in its other activities is equally unconstitutional, as I understand the establishment clause. . . . The First Amendment does not say that some form of establishment is allowed; it says that 'no law respecting an establishment of religion' shall be made. What may not be done directly may not be done indirectly, lest the establishment clause become a mockery."

Never has the wall of separation between church and state been raised higher than in the concurring opinions of Justice Douglas.

The only possible conclusion is that his views have changed drastically in the decade between *Zorach* and *Engle*.

Other Justices, notably Justice Brennan in *Abington Township*, sought to state that Douglas' view was not theirs. Then there is the view of Justice Reed in his dissent in *McCullum:* "The prohibition of enactments respecting the establishment of religion does not bar every friendly gesture between church and state. It is not an absolute prohibition against every conceivable situation where the two may work together. . . ."

Justice Brennan said in his concurring opinion in *Abington v. Schempp,* "I cannot accept the contention . . . that every involvement of religion in public life violates the establishment clause." He sought particularly to say that he did not believe tax exemptions for churches are unconstitutional.

There is no doubt that certain church organizations view with alarm the opinion expressed by Justice Douglas in his concurring opinions in the school-prayer cases. If his view prevails, it could have a most significant effect on religious practice in the United States.

There also can be no doubt that there are those who would like to have his views written into law. Cases have already been brought challenging the constitutionality of grants and other forms of financial aid to church-affiliated colleges (state courts in Maryland recently declared such aid illegal), of exemptions from federal income taxes granted to church-owned businesses, of exemptions to property taxes most churches enjoy, of tax deductions allowed on monies given to churches.

The effect of these actions, if won, would be staggering. Isolated studies show that churches may own 2 to 5 per cent of all taxable property in the United States and that real-estate tax revenues might increase 3 to 6 per cent if churches were taxed. Another study postulates that churches own 14 per cent of all taxable property in Pennsylvania, 17 per cent in Maryland and 18 per cent in New Jersey. A third study estimates that the Catholic Church owns tax-exempt property in the United States worth $11 billion, including 38 per cent of the tax-exempt property of Washington, D.C.

If churches were forced to pay taxes, many feel that the poorer churches would be forced to close. Others believe large church buildings would become impractical. Certainly many church educational and charitable activities would be curtailed, and at least one church leader believes the forms of worship would be altered as taxation forced churches to economize on buildings and to curtail expensive pomp and ceremony.

The roots of these judicial cases have been the subject of ecclesiastical discussions which have been going on for many years. A number of prominent churchmen have spoken out on the subject. Dr. Eugene Carson Blake, leading executive of the United Presbyterian Church and past president of the National Council of Churches, wrote in a widely quoted article in *Christianity Today*, "The economic power that will increasingly be wielded by ever-richer churches threatens to produce not only envy, hatred or resentment of non-members, but also to distort the purposes of church members and leaders themselves. . . ."

The *Cumberland Presbyterian Magazine* wrote, "The church should consider withdrawing from the 'favored position' it holds in relation to taxation." *Together,* official organ of the Methodist Church, said, "Serious questions have been raised about religion's traditional tax-exempt status" which have "practical and moral—as well as legal—aspects." Two Episcopal churchmen have urged America's churches to start paying their fair share of government and community costs and end the traditional "free tax ride." And Dr. Blake, warning of possible "revolutionary expropriation of church properties," says, "History makes it clear that social welfare and educational enterprises by the churches, however much appreciated, are not sufficient of themselves to make a poor man love a rich church."

Many studies have been made of church-owned, profit-making, tax-exempt business enterprises. Almost no religious sect is without them. Recent studies showed that Temple Baptist Church in Los Angeles owned the Auditorium Office Building and Philharmonic Auditorium. The Biltmore Hotel in Dayton, Ohio, was owned by Christian, Baptist and Presbyterian churches in Bloomington, Illinois. A New Hampshire Congregational church operated a laundry. The First Methodist Church of Chicago owned and worshiped in a twenty-two-story office building. The Seventh-Day Adventists owned the Loma Linda Food Company in California. The Mormon

Church owned and operated a newspaper, radio and television stations, hotel, banks and hundreds of farms, including one in Florida with 740,000 acres and 100,000 cattle. St. Andrews Catholic Church in Chicago owned the Hollywood Roosevelt and the Sacramento El Rancho hotels. The Jesuit Order owned WWL Radio and TV in New Orleans. The full list would be quite long.

Many church leaders are outspoken in criticism of this. Said Egidio Cardinal Vagnozzi, when he was Apostolic Delegate to the United States, "Sound and prudent financing is necessary, but concern with finances should not be allowed to turn religious superiors into businessmen and religious institutions into corporations." The *Christian Science Monitor* has called for revision of federal tax laws "to prevent American taxpayers from having in effect to subsidize religious forays into the competitive market place." Warned C. Emanuel Carlson, executive director of the Baptist Joint Committee on Public Affairs, "If it should be demonstrated that the vast efforts now carried forward by the churches are really powered by American tax policies rather than by commitments to God, then churches are already dependent on public policy . . . [and are] in line for a national rather than a prophetic role."

Judges and justices searching for the "dominant opinion" on the delicate questions of church-operated businesses and church tax exemptions cannot help but be made aware of these and other similar views.

The intention here is not to express a dominant view but to indicate that there are those prominent church leaders who disagree or at least have mixed feelings about long-standing governmental attitudes toward tax exemptions for churches and other financial aids mentioned by Justice Douglas.

What is being said here is that the Supreme Court and the American people have not heard the last—by far—of the cases dealing with religion in American life. For many years to come these matters, as well as others undreamed of, may come before the high court, challenging the judgment of the Justices, the wisdom of all Americans, and the practice of religion in our lives. Truly this is one of the great issues to come before the Court in our lifetime.

IX. JUSTICE IS FOR EVERYONE

We hold . . . that when . . . the suspect has requested and been denied an opportunity to consult with his lawyer . . . that no statement elicited by the police during the interrogation may be used against him at a criminal trial.—Justice Arthur J. Goldberg for the Court in ESCOBEDO V. ILLINOIS

Law enforcement may have the element of a contest about it, but it is not a game.—Justice Byron R. White, dissenting in MASSIAH V. U.S.

In 1942 the Justices of the Supreme Court listened to arguments concerning Smith Betts, a farm hand in Carroll County, northwest of Baltimore, Maryland. The question under consideration was whether Betts, who had been charged with robbery, had received a fair trial.

Betts had asked the Carroll County Court to appoint an attorney to plead his case, explaining that he was too poor to hire his own attorney. The Maryland judge refused, saying the practice was to appoint lawyers for the poor only for crimes bearing the death penalty. Since robbery carried only a prison sentence, even though a long one, Betts would have to be his own attorney.

Betts had done a creditable job as his own, makeshift counsel. He had cross-examined witnesses called by the prosecution and subpoenaed some witnesses in his own defense. But to no avail. He was found guilty and sentenced to eight years in prison. From behind bars Betts filed a petition for *habeas corpus* with Chief Judge

Carroll T. Bond of Maryland's Court of Appeals, contending that Carroll County's refusal to provide him with a lawyer violated his constitutional rights.

Judge Bond, a highly respected jurist, reviewed the case. It was a simple trial, he found, consisting of identification of Betts and his alibi. Betts had done a fairly good job. He was forty-three years old, intelligent, and he had experience, for he had been in a criminal court once before. He had pleaded guilty to larceny and served a sentence.

For all these reasons Judge Bond ruled against Betts, saying, "In this case it must be said there was little for counsel to do on either side."

When the case came to the Supreme Court the result seemed a foregone conclusion. After all, the Court had only ten years before, in one of its landmark cases (*Powell v. Alabama*, 287 U.S. 45), ruled that poor, helpless defendants were entitled to court-appointed counsel in cases bearing the death penalty. Only four years before, in *Johnson v. Zerbst* (304 U.S. 458), the Court held that in federal courts every defendant had a right to counsel at his trial. The majority opinion was written by that indefatigible defender of individual rights, Justice Black.

With this record, who could doubt that the high court would now require all defendants in state courts, whether charged with a capital crime or not, be provided an attorney? Regardless of who could doubt it, the Court, by a 6–3 vote, upset the predictors and ruled against Betts.

Said Justice Roberts for the Court, ". . . in the great majority of the states, it has been the considered judgment of the people, their representatives and their courts that appointment of counsel is not a fundamental right, essential to a fair trail. On the contrary, the matter has generally been deemed one of legislative policy. . . . The states should not be straitjacketed. . . ."

Only one guess is needed to know who dissented: Justice Black. Joined by Justices Douglas and Murphy, he termed the right to counsel "fundamental," saying, "Any other practice seems to me to defeat the promise of our democratic society to provide equal justice under the law."

Few liked the decision. Particularly in the legal profession *Betts v.*

Brady was widely condemned. The Court itself "bent over backwards" to get around it. This was done by determining that the defendant had not received a fair trial for reasons other than his lack of counsel.

Betts v. Brady was still on the books on August 4, 1961, when Clarence Earl Gideon went on trial in the Circuit Court of the Fourteenth Judicial Circuit in Florida. Gideon's case has been reported in detail, notably in Anthony Lewis' excellent book *Gideon's Trumpet*. Gideon, fifty-one, was charged with breaking and entering a pool hall in Panama City, Florida, and stealing an undetermined amount of money from vending machines and some liquor.

Gideon asked the court to appoint a counsel for him. His request was refused, on the grounds provided in *Betts v. Brady.* Gideon acted as his own lawyer, did a reasonably good job, but not reasonably good enough. He was convicted and sentenced to five years in prison. From there he asked the Court to review his case. The Court agreed and appointed as his attorney Abe Fortas, a top Washington attorney, who is now Mr. Justice Fortas, named by President Johnson to succeeed Justice Goldberg in 1965.

The appointment of Mr. Fortas to represent Gideon, as well as other factors about the case, foretold that the Court was about to reverse *Betts v. Brady.* Mr. Fortas made powerful arguments, both in brief and orally. Leading attorneys submitted arguments as friends of the Court. A large number of state law officials, who would predictably have approved of *Betts v. Brady* as a defense of states' rights, came out for its reversal. The Justice Department wanted the precedent overruled.

Decision in *Gideon v. Wainwright* (373 U.S. 335) came on March 18, 1963. ". . . reason and reflection," said the Court opinion, "require us to recognize that in our adversary system of criminal justice, any person haled into court, who is too poor to hire a lawyer, cannot be assured a fair trial unless counsel is provided for him. This seems to us to be an obvious truth. Government, both state and federal, quite properly spends vast sums of money to establish machinery to try defendants accused of crime. Lawyers to prosecute are everywhere deemed essential to protect the public's interest in an orderly society. Similarly, there are few defendants charged with crime, few indeed, who fail to hire the best lawyers they can get to prepare and present their defenses. That governments hire lawyers to prosecute and defendants who have the money hire lawyers to defend are the strongest indications of the widespread belief that lawyers in criminal courts are necessities, not luxuries. The right of one charged with crime to counsel may not be deemed fundamental and essential to fair trials in some countries, but it is in ours."

The words are those of Justice Black, who in twenty-one years saw his powerful dissent in *Betts v. Brady* become law in *Gideon v. Wainwright*.

This decision has brought and is bringing great changes in the law. Machinery is being set up to provide indigent defendants with counsel. Our whole attitude is being changed to the viewpoint that the poverty-stricken should have equal justice with the rich and powerful.

Gideon v. Wainwright also serves to dramatize a problem with which the Supreme Court is now wrestling, a problem which may be battled through the courts for years to come.

The question has probably already occurred to you. If a man has a right to counsel, when does that right begin? At his trial, surely, but when does his trial begin? Does his right to counsel begin when he is indicted, when he is charged by police—or earlier? Does it begin when police question him at the station house?

These are vital questions and extremely difficult to answer. The decisions made by the courts can change the face of America. Let's look at the opposing viewpoints:

Suppose a man enters a grocery store, pulls a gun and demands the contents of the cash register. The proprietor refuses. The gunman shoots the grocer, scoops up the money and runs out. Police arrive, determined to protect citizens from this killer-bandit. From witnesses who saw the gunman run out of the store, police obtain his description. One witness says he believes the bandit was John Smith, who is picked up by police and taken to the station house. When questioned, Smith denies any knowledge of the crime. Police do not believe him and continue to question him. Several hours later, when confronted with the witnesses against him, Smith confesses to the crime.

From one viewpoint this is excellent police work. Detectives have solved a crime; they have removed from society a gunman and bandit who has already shot one man. They have prevented him from shooting others. By persistent questioning they have gotten him to admit the error of his ways and to confess.

From another viewpoint, Smith's rights have been invaded. He was snatched from his home, taken to a police station, surrounded by uniformed men and held incommunicado until he confessed, and thereby surrendered his constitutionally guaranteed right not to testify against himself or to incriminate himself. The whole process smacks of fascist, Nazi, Communist, totalitarian, secret-police methods by which individual freedom has been destroyed in much of the world.

These are the twin shoals the Supreme Court must navigate as it supervises the administration of justice in this land: the needs of society to enforce obedience to its laws and to protect the constitutional liberties of all citizens.

Actually, the problem, as stated in the Smith analogy, is an oversimplification. Let's suppose that Smith is not a foolish young man who decides, on impulse, to rob a grocery store. Let's suppose he is a hardened, professional criminal, a member of an international criminal organization who shot the grocer because he refused to buy his bread or meat or soft drinks from firms owned by the criminal organization. Such "sale" of merchandise is extorted on a regular basis in many large cities, so the example is hardly hypothetical. In detaining Smith until he confessed, police were not only catching a murderer; they were also combatting a powerful criminal organization which was spawning lawlessness all over the country. Was this wrong?

Or let's suppose that Smith was a member of a subversive organization advocating the revolutionary overthrow of the government. Were police wrong in detaining him?

Many thoughtful people would answer: yes, this was wrong. Our constitutional liberties must be protected. Suppose Smith were innocent of all these charges. Suppose he was wrongly identified and confessed simply because he was afraid or tired or confused. Or, it is maintained, that even though Smith may be guilty, that fact cannot legalize law-enforcement techniques which might be used against Jones, who is innocent.

For decades the arguments in behalf of society's rights to have laws enforced were dominant. Betts was only one of many men and women jailed under this justification. However, it should be noted that protection of society was not the only reason the Betts conviction was upheld. The issue also involved states' rights: that the state, because it is closer to the people, need not be as restricted as the federal courts, more distant, should be. The argument continues that the Fourteenth Amendment is not a catch-all, imposing the same limitations on states as on the federal government. In recent years the Supreme Court has been moving to afford greater protection to individual rights, thereby throttling, some believe, the states'-rights tradition.

Gideon v. Wainwright was one of these steps. A man is entitled to an attorney at his trial—if he asks for one. What if he doesn't ask for one? Should the judge provide him with one anyhow, so that no one is tried without an attorney in any criminal case? This question, at this writing, has not been answered. Most lawyers think the Court will say, "Yes."

Is a defendant entitled to advice of counsel at any time prior to his trial? The Court has already answered "Yes." In 1959 it ruled, in *Sprano v. New York* (360 U.S. 315), that police could not obtain a confession from a man already under indictment unless he had an attorney representing him. In this case, Sprano, after his indictment, was taken to the police station and questioned. He signed a confession. The high court ruled that the confession was inadmissible at his trial because Sprano lacked a lawyer.

In 1964 the high court went a step further on this question in the fascinating case of *Massiah v. U.S.* (377 U.S. 201). In 1959 United States customs agents learned that Winston Massiah, a member of the crew of the SS *Santa Maria*, was transporting narcotics aboard that ship as it journeyed from a South American port to the United States. At New York, agents boarded the *Santa Maria* and found five packages containing 3½ pounds of cocaine. Massiah was arrested, arraigned and indicted for possession of narcotics aboard a U.S. vessel.

After his indictment and while awaiting trial, Massiah was released on bail. He met Jesse Colson, who had been arrested as Massiah's co-defendant. They went for a ride in Colson's car and

Massiah talked at length about his part in the conspiracy. He made a number of statements which incriminated himself. What Massiah didn't know was that Colson had turned "stool pigeon." He had agreed to cooperate with federal agents. In fact, an electronic recording device was installed by Agent Finlarr Murphy under the seat of Colson's car. Agent Murphy, following in another car, was able to overhear every one of Massiah's incriminating words.

At Massiah's trial, Murphy was permitted to testify about what Massiah had said in Colson's car. Massiah was convicted and sentenced to nine years in prison.

The issue before the Supreme Court was whether Massiah's statements to Colson as overheard by Murphy could be used against him. On May 18, 1964, the Court, divided 6–3, ruled for Massiah. Justice Stewart wrote a short, to-the-point opinion.

"We hold," he said, "that the petitioner [Massiah] was denied the basic protection of that guarantee [aid of counsel] when there was used against him at his trial evidence of his own incriminating words which federal agents had deliberately elicited from him after he had been indicted and in the absence of his counsel. It is true that in the *Sprano* case, the defendant was interrogated in a police station, where here the damaging testimony was elicited from the defendant without his knowledge while he was 'free on bail.' . . .

"We do not question that in this case, as in many cases, it was entirely proper to continue an investigation of the suspected criminal activities of the defendant and his alleged confederate, even though the defendant had already been indicted. All that we hold is that the defendant's own incriminating statements, obtained by federal agents under the circumstances here disclosed, could not constitutionally be introduced by the prosecution as evidence against *him* at his trail."

In other words, police are permitted to continue the investigation after an indictment, even "bugging" an accused's car. They can use the information obtained to make other investigations and arrests, but they cannot use the information at the accused's trial.

Massiah brought a sharp dissent from a new, powerful voice on the bench, Justice Byron "Whizzer" White. Former college football star at the University of Colorado, former Rhodes Scholar, former All-Pro Halfback in the National Football League, he became an outstanding lawyer and Deputy Attorney General in the Kennedy Administration. He was named to the Supreme Court in 1962, a widely acclaimed appointment. Justice White has shown himself to be a consistent voice in support of law enforcement and a powerful writer of dissenting opinions. In *Massiah* he was joined by Justices Clark and Harlan.

"In my view, a civilized society must maintain its capacity to discover transgressors of the law and to identify those who flout it. . . . It will just not do to sweep these disagreeable matters under the rug or to pretend they are not there at all. It is therefore a rather portentous occasion when a constitutional rule is established barring the use of evidence which is relevant, reliable and highly probative of the issue which the trial court has before it—whether the accused committed the act with which he is charged. Without the evidence, the quest for truth may be seriously impeded and in many cases the trial court, although aware of proof showing defendant's guilt, must nevertheless release him because the criminal evidence is deemed inadmissible. . . .

"I am unable to see how this case presents an unconstitutional interference with Massiah's right to counsel. Massiah was not prevented from consulting with counsel as often as he wished. No meetings with counsel were disturbed or spied upon. Preparations for trial were in no way obstructed. . . . This is nothing more than a thinly disguised constitutional policy of minimizing or entirely prohibiting the use in evidence of voluntary out-of-court admissions and confessions made by the accused. Carried as far as blind logic may compel some to go, the notion that statements from the mouths of the defendant should not be used in evidence would have a severe and unfortunate impact upon the great bulk of cases. . . .

"Until now the Court has expressly rejected the argument that admissions are to be deemed involuntary if made outside the presence of counsel. At the time of the conversation in question, petitioner was not in custody but free on bail. He was not questioned in what anyone could call an atmosphere of official coercion. What he said was said to his partner in crime who had also been indicted. There was no suggestion or any possibility of coercion. . . ."

Justice White pointed out that if Colson had not prearranged the interview with Agent Murphy but had gone to agents and told them what Massiah had said—and even brought a recording of it—that would have been admissible. Then Justice White got to the heart of his argument:

"Reporting criminal behavior is expected or even demanded of the ordinary citizen. Friends may be subpoenaed to testify about friends, relatives about relatives and partners about partners. I therefore question the soundness of insulating Massiah from the apostasy of his partner in crime and of furnishing constitutional sanction for the strike secrecy and discipline of criminal organizations." What he referred to was the "code of the underworld" that members never "squeal" on other members.

"Neither the ordinary citizen nor the confessed criminal should be discouraged from reporting what he knows to the authorities and from lending his aid to secure evidence of crime. Certainly after this case the Colsons will be few and far between; the Massiahs can breathe much more easily, secure in the knowledge that the Constitution furnishes an important measure of protection against faithless compatriots and guarantees sporting treatment for sporting peddlers of narcotics.

"Meanwhile, of course, the public will again be the loser and law enforcement will be presented with another serious dilemma. When police have arrested and released on bail one member of a criminal ring and another member, a confederate, is cooperating with police, can the confederate be allowed to continue his association with the ring or must he somehow be withdrawn to avoid challenge to trial evidence on the ground that it was acquired after, rather than before, the arrest, after, rather than, before the indictment? . . .

"Here there was no substitution of brutality for brain, no inherent charge of police coercion. . . . Massiah was not being interrogated in a police station, was not surrounded by numerous officers or questioned in relays and was not forbidden access to others. Law enforcement may have the element of a contest about it, but it is not a game."

Justice White's dissent is quoted in greater length here, not because it is necessarily more correct than that of the Court majority but rather because it is such an excellent statement of the traditional or "conservative" views of prosecutors and law-enforcement officials.

There can be no doubt that *Massiah* makes the job of police and prosecutors much more difficult. The "jail-house stoolie," long a favorite police weapon, has been put under some restrictions, to say the least.

Many questions remain, such as whether the stoolie can testify if he had not previously made arrangements with police. The Supreme Court will surely be asked to settle that one.

A month and four days after *Massiah*, the Court rendered a decision of epoch proportions in its effect on law enforcement.

On January 19, 1960, Danny Escobedo, a twenty-two-year-old of Mexican extraction, was arrested about 2:30 A.M. without a warrant by Chicago police, who wanted to question him about the fatal shooting of his brother-in-law eleven days before. Escobedo made no statement to police, and about 5 P.M. he was released on a writ of *habeas corpus* obtained by his lawyer, Warren Wolfson. A writ of *habeas corpus*, known as "The Great Writ" because of its importance, protects free men from imprisonment without cause and fair trial.

On January 30, Benedict DiGerlando, then in police custody and who was later indicted for murder, told police that Escobedo had fired the fatal shots. Between eight and nine that night, Escobedo and his sister, the widow of the murder victim, were picked up and taken to police headquarters. En route to the station, police handcuffed Escobedo's hands behind his back and one of the policemen told him that DiGerlando had named him as the one who fired the murder shot.

Escobedo later testified that detectives told him he "might as well admit the crime," but that he replied, "I am sorry, but I would like to have advice from my lawyer."

Almost simultaneously, attorney Wolfson was on his way to the Detective Bureau, where Escobedo was being kept. He described his efforts to help Escobedo in this way:

"On that day I received a phone call [from a person other than Escobedo] and . . . I went to the Detective Bureau at 11th and State. The first person I talked to was the sergeant on duty at the Bureau desk, Sergeant Pidgeon. I asked Sergeant Pidgeon for permission to speak to my client, Danny Escobedo. . . . Sergeant Pidgeon made a call to the Bureau lockup and informed me that the boy had been taken from the lockup to the Homicide Bureau. This was between 9:30 and 10:00 in the evening. Before I went any-where, he [Sergeant Pidgeon] called the Homicide Bureau and told them there was an attorney wanting to see Escobedo. He told me I could not see him. Then I went upstairs to the Homicide Bureau.

"There were several homicide detectives around. I talked to them. I identified myself as Escobedo's attorney and asked permission to see him. They said I could not. . . . The police officer told me to see Chief Flynn, who was on duty. I identified myself to Chief Flynn and asked permission to see my client. He said I could not. . . . I think it was approximately 11 o'clock. He said I couldn't see him because they hadn't completed questioning. . . . For a second or two I spotted him [Escobedo] in the homicide bureau. The door was open and I could see through the office. . . . I waved to him and he waved back and then the door was closed by one of the officers. . . ."

Escobedo testified that he interpreted Wolfson's wave to mean that he was to say nothing.

The attorney continued: "There were four or five officers milling around the Homicide Bureau that night. . . . I waited around for another hour or two and went back again and renewed [my] request to see my client. Chief Flynn again told me I could not. . . . I filed an official complaint with Commissioner Phelan of the Chicago Police Department. I had a conversation with every police officer I could find. I was told at Homicide that I could not see him and I would have to obtain a writ of *habeas corpus*. I left the Homicide Bureau and from the Detective Bureau . . . at approxi-mately 1 A.M. I had no opportunity to talk to my client that night."

Meanwhile, as Wolfson was making his frantic efforts to help his client, Escobedo was being talked to by a Spanish-speaking officer who knew Escobedo's family. Escobedo claimed that the officer told him that if he made a statement against DiGerlando, he could go home, and that is why he made his statement. The officer denied making any such promise.

In any event, Escobedo and DiGerlando were brought together. Escobedo looked at DiGerlando and blurted, "I didn't shoot Manuel, you did it."

In this way Danny Escobedo admitted knowing of the crime. An Assistant State's Attorney, Theodore J. Cooper, was brought in to ask "carefully framed questions apparently designed to insure their admissibility into evidence." Cooper did not inform Escobedo of his constitutional rights, nor did anyone else during the interrogation. Escobedo was convicted and sentenced to life.

The issue of whether Escobedo was wrongly denied access to his lawyer went to the Supreme Court, which divided in its decision in *Escobedo v. Illinois* (378 U.S. 478). The five-man majority consisted of Chief Justice Warren and Justices Black, Douglas, Brennan and Goldberg, who wrote the decision—in favor of Escobedo.

"When petitioner [Escobedo] requested and was denied an opportunity to consult with his lawyer, the investigation had ceased to be a general investigation of 'an unsolved crime.' Petitioner had become the accused and the purpose of the interrogation was to 'get him' to confess his guilt despite his constitutional right not to do so."

Then Justice Goldberg said, "We have learned the lesson of history, ancient and modern, that a system of criminal law enforcement which consistently relies on the 'confession' will, in the long run, be less reliable and more subject to abuses than a system which depends on extrinsic evidence independently secured through skillful investigation.

"We hold, therefore, that when, as here, the investigation is no longer a general inquiry into an unsolved crime but has begun to focus on a particular suspect, the suspect has been taken into police custody, the police carry out a process of interrogation that lends itself to eliciting incriminating statements, the suspect has requested and been denied an opportunity to consult with his lawyer, and the police have not effectively warned him of his absolute constitutional right to remain silent, the accused has been denied the 'assistance of counsel' in violation of the Sixth Amendment to the Constitution . . . and that no statement elicited by the police during the interrogation may be used against him at a criminal trial."

The dissents were bitter and biting. Justice Harlan: "I think the rule announced today is most ill-conceived and that it seriously and unjustfully fetters perfectly legitimate methods of criminal law enforcement."

Justice Stewart: "The confession that the Court today holds inadmissible was a voluntary one. It was given during the course of a perfectly legitimate police investigation of an unsolved murder. The Court says that what happened during this investigation 'affected' the trial. I had always supposed the whole purpose of a police investigation of a murder was to 'affect' the trial of the murderer and that it would be only an incomplete, unsuccessful or corrupt investigation which would not do so."

Justice Stewart said he felt that the Court opinion "perverts . . . precious constitutional guarantees."

Again it was Justice White who made the strongest dissent, in which Justices Clark and Stewart joined: "At the very least the Court holds that once the accused becomes a suspect, presumably is arrested, any admission made to the police thereafter is inadmissible in evidence unless the accused has waived his right to counsel. The decision is thus another major step in the direction of the goal which the Court seemingly has in mind—to bar from evidence all admissions obtained from an individual suspected of crime, whether involuntarily made or not. . . .

"By abandoning the voluntary-involuntary rule for admissibility of confessions, the Court seems driven by the notion that it is uncivilized law enforcement to use an accused's own admissions against him at his trial. . . . The right to counsel now not only entitles the accused to counsel's advice and aid in preparing for trial, but stands as an impenetrable barrier to any interrogation once the accused has become a suspect. From that very moment, apparently, his right to counsel attaches, a rule wholly unworkable and impossible to administer unless police cars are equipped with public defenders and undercover agents and police informants have defense counsels at their side. . . .

"Under this new rule one might just as well argue that a potential defendant is constitutionally entitled to a lawyer before, not after, he commits a crime, since it is then that crucial incriminating evidence is put within the reach of the government by the would-be accused. Until now there simply has been no right guaranteed by the Federal Constitution to be free from the use at trial of a voluntary admission made prior to indictment. . . .

"Furthermore, until now, the Constitution has permitted the accused to be fingerprinted and to be identified in a line-up or in the courtroom itself. The Court chooses to ignore these matters and to rely on the virtue and morality of a system of criminal law enforcement which does not depend on the 'confession.' No such judgment is to be found in the Constitution. . . . The only 'inquisition' the Constitution forbids are those which compel incrimination. Escobedo's statements were not compelled, and the Court does not hold that they were.

"Obviously law enforcement officers can make mistakes and exceed their authority, as today's decision shows that even judges can do, but I have somewhat more faith than the Court evidently has in the ability and desire of prosecution and of the power of the appellate courts to discern and correct such violations of the law. . . .

"I do not suggest for a moment that law enforcement will be destroyed by the rule announced today. The need for peace and order is too insistent for that. But it will be crippled and its task made a great deal more difficult—all, in my opinion, for unsound, unstated reasons which can find no home in any provision of the Constitution."

Escobedo was greeted with a roar of outraged indignation by the nation's prosecutors. "Someday, I guess," said one, "the Court will rule that we can't talk to a suspect without first giving him a lawyer. When that happens, believe me, the ball game is over. You're going to see a lot of killers and rapists walking out of police stations with thumb to noses. We shall see how the public will like that."

James C. Crumlish, Jr., district attorney of Philadelphia, said in commenting on a spate of holdup-murders in the City of Brotherly Love, "I am convinced these killings were spawned by the Court's liberal interpretation of the Constitution. A thief knows that his chances of electrocution and long sentences are remote, so he risks killing the victim of the robbery. That way he destroys the evidence against him—often the only evidence we have."

Many leaped to praise the Court. Professors Gerhard O. W. Mueller and Patrick M. Wall of New York University, writing in the *Annual Survey of American Law*, said, " . . . we continue to demand and praise continued humanization of American criminal law."

To say *Escobedo* was a bombshell is to make a gross understatement. Everyone had an idea what it meant, but no one could be sure. Supporters of customary police practices gave the decision a narrow interpretation, insisting it applied only to the special circumstances of the *Escobedo* case. More liberal attorneys, judges and law professors viewed the decision as forcing a broad change in police practices, in which suspects must be advised of their rights, provided with an attorney, and promptly arraigned with or without police interrogation. Liberals were encouraged by *Escobedo* to believe that all confessions might be declared illegal, that no man could be questioned by police without his lawyer being present, and much more.

The interpreters of *Escobedo* squared off into camps. The questions became court issues, and lower courts were asked to rule— and they ruled both ways. On the question of whether a confession was valid if the suspect was not informed of his right to call an attorney, for example, courts of equal rank in California and Pennsylvania ruled such confessions were invalid, while similar courts in Illinois and New York ruled that they were valid. So great was the confusion that the Chief Justice of New Jersey, confronted with opposite rulings by federal appellate courts in Philadelphia and New York, ordered courts of his state to ignore both and abide by state law.

For two years the Supreme Court let the "pot boil." It refused to review the conflicting decision, while the argument over *Escobedo* was waged in bar journals, bar associations and in the public press. This action (or inaction) by the Court was a clear example of its providing time for the formation of a dominant opinion. Then in 1965 the Court accepted several cases for review, and in its next to last day of its session in June 1966 began clarifying its intent in *Escobedo*.

There were four cases embodied in the rulings, the principal one being *Miranda v. Arizona*. The opinion was by Chief Justice Warren, indicating the importance of the cases. With one exception the majority was 5–4, with Justice Fortas taking the place of former Justice Goldberg in the majority.

The Court ruled that a prosecutor cannot use in a trial any admissions or confessions made by a suspect while in custody unless it first proves that the police complied with detailed safeguards to protect the defendant's rights against self-incrimination. The suspect must be clearly warned that he may remain silent, that anything he says may be used against him and that he has a right to have a lawyer present during questioning. If the suspect desires a lawyer but cannot afford one, he cannot be questioned unless a court-appointed attorney is present. If the suspect confesses after receiving the required warnings but without counsel, the burden is on the prosecution to prove he knew what he was doing when he waived his right. Any prolonged interrogation will be taken to show a lack of waiver. Moreover, if the suspect makes a waiver of rights, then asks to see a lawyer, all questioning must stop until he sees one. If the suspect goes it alone but indicates "in any manner" that he wants to remain silent, the police must stop interrogating him.

The decision might be characterized as left of center on the issue. It did not specifically rule out the use of confessions in evidence. It did not rule out questioning of witnesses at the scene of a crime or detention of a suspect while his story was being checked out. Nor did it require the presence of lawyers at police stations. Spontaneous admissions of guilt can be offered as evidence, as long as they do not come after illegal interrogation without counsel.

But the rulings obviously necessitate great changes in police procedure. Interrogation of a suspect to gain evidence or a confession is obviously vastly more difficult. If the suspect wishes to say nothing, interrogation must stop. If he wants a lawyer present during questioning, one must be provided him and the lawyer has a right, indeed a duty, to advise the suspect to say nothing. If the suspect waives his rights, the police must prove he did so voluntarily. Nor can police circumvent the intent of the ruling by questioning the suspect in the police car on the way to the station house or use other ruses.

As with *Massiah* and *Escobedo*, the majority was scored by dissenters. Justice Harlan, in a voice filled with emotion, denounced the decision as "dangerous experimentation" at a time of a "high crime rate that is a matter of growing concern." Justice White said, "In some unknown number of cases the Court's rule will return a killer, a rapist or other criminal to the streets and to the environment which produced him, to repeat his crime whenever it pleases him. As a consequence, there will not be a gain, but a loss, in human dignity."

The fears expressed by the dissenters, police officers and prosecutors that the decision would compel the release of thousands of convicted prisoners were negated the following day when the Court ruled that its decisions were not retroactive.

It is possible to predict several results from these decisions. First, the issues are far from settled. The "answers" in *Miranda* provoked a new spate of questions: What is the meaning of custody? What constitutes proof a defendant waived his rights? If a confession was illegally obtained, can the fruits of it be used in evidence? Criminal procedure will remain an issue in the Marble Palace for many years.

Second, changes in police procedure will be necessary. Use of confessions as evidence will be sharply curtailed, while use of physical evidence such as fingerprints, laboratory analysis, etc., is greatly expanded. (The search for physical evidence was strengthened when the Court ruled a defendant may not balk at giving a sample of his blood to determine if he was drunk while driving.) There may be periods of adjustment in which the police make many errors, but the end result cannot help but be greater humanization of police procedure to protect individual liberties.

Third, whether the fears that police efforts to control crime are so hampered as to increase crime are justified remains to be seen. If police are handicapped and if crime increases as a result, it is not unreasonable to expect the Court to reconsider these decisions, especially since they are 5–4 cases.

Fourth, these decisions certainly mean a whole new direction for law enforcement in this country. But before we discuss that, let's first look at some other areas of criminal procedure where the Court has upset old methods.

X. LAW ENFORCEMENT AND JUSTICE IN CONFLICT

There is no war between the Constitution and common sense.
—Justice Tom C. Clark for the Court in MAPP V. OHIO

Our Constitution assumes the common sense of the people . . .
—Justice Hugo L. Black, dissenting in BARENBLATT V. U.S.

There are valid reasons for criminals to think that crime does pay and that slow and fumbling justice can be evaded.—Lewis F. Powell, past president of the American Bar Association

On May 23, 1957, a trio of Cleveland, Ohio, police officers went to the home of Miss Dollree Mapp on the second floor of a duplex house. The policemen were following information that persons were hiding in Miss Mapp's home who had information about a recent bombing. They also believed there was a large amount of "policy paraphernalia"—that is, slips of paper, tally sheets and other material used in the numbers racket—hidden in her home.

Miss Mapp, who lived there with her fifteen-year-old daughter by a previous marriage, called her attorney, and he advised her to ask the policemen for a search warrant. When she learned they had none, she refused to admit them.

The officers remained outside—in police terminology they "kept the house under surveillance"—for three hours, and then four more officers joined them. Again they went to the door and knocked.

When Miss Mapp did not come to the door immediately, they forced the door and entered. They found Miss Mapp halfway down the stairs from the upper floor, rather obviously on her way to the door. She demanded to see their search warrant. A paper which police said was a warrant was held up to her. She grabbed the "warrant" and placed it in the bosom of her dress. A struggle ensued, in which the officers recovered the piece of paper. Miss Mapp was handcuffed because she was "belligerent" in resisting the official rescue of the "warrant from her person."

"Running roughshod over appellant, a policeman 'grabbed her, twisted [her] hand,' and she 'yelled [and] pleaded with him' because 'it was hurting.'" Still in handcuffs, Miss Mapp was forcibly taken upstairs to her bedroom, where the officers searched a dresser, a chest, drawers, a closet and some suitcases. They also looked into a photograph album and through personal papers belonging to Miss Mapp. The search spread to the rest of the second floor, including the child's bedroom, the living room, the kitchen and a dinette, the basement of the building and a trunk found there. Police found some pamphlets and photographs which they contended were pornographic.

Miss Mapp was arrested and charged under Ohio law forbidding possession of obscene materials. She insisted the materials belonged to a former roomer who had left the trunk there, but she was convicted. The matter went to the Ohio Supreme Court, which ruled 4–3 that the law under which she was convicted was unconstitutional. Under Ohio law, however, a state statute cannot be declared void if more than one state Supreme Court Justice votes to uphold it. Since three had, the law and Miss Mapp's conviction stood.

The case went to the Supreme Court as *Mapp v. Ohio* (367 U.S. 643) and was argued March 29, 1961. The question of whether Ohio's law violated Miss Mapp's right to free speech and free thought was vigorously argued. The question of whether Miss Mapp's home had been illegally entered and searched and whether she was convicted on the basis of illegally seized evidence was not mentioned by her lawyers, either orally or in written briefs.

The decision, rendered on June 19, 1961, by Justice Clark is viewed by many as one of the more surprising ones in recent Court history. First surprise was that Justice Clark wrote it. A former practicing attorney, county and government prosecutor and United States Attorney General, he has consistently advocated a strong judiciary and strong law enforcement. He has been the leader in the group of justices who believe society's need for protection is paramount and the individual must surrender some "rights" to society's requirements.

Now this friend of law enforcement came out strongly against the police methods used in the Mapp case and held that states could not use illegally seized evidence at a trial. Much of the language used in the description of the arrest of Miss Mapp earlier in this chapter comes from Justice Clark's opinion, making it quite readable.

Lawyers were surprised by the split on the case. Justice Clark was joined by Chief Justice Warren and Justices Brennan, Black and Stewart. Justice Douglas wrote an opinion agreeing with the reversal of Miss Mapp's conviction, but on different grounds. Justices Harlan, Frankfurter and Whittaker dissented. What caused lawyers to raise eyebrows was that Justice Black concurred with Justice Clark only in part, leaving some points of the decision to rest on less than a majority of the Court.

What is astounding is that the Court made such a revolutionary opinion on such a shaky majority and that it—in the words of the dissenters—"reached" so far to make the decision. As we noted before, major reversals of Court thinking are often forseeable. A number of decisions foreshadow the final overturning of a major precedent. The decision in *Mapp v. Ohio* was a sort of judicial bolt from the blue.

Overturned was *Wolf v. Colorado* (338 U.S. 25), a controversial opinion of 1949. In substance, the Court had ruled in *Wolf* that the Fourteenth Amendment does not forbid a prosecutor in a state court from using illegally seized evidence against a defendant. Other Supreme Court decisions forbid *federal* prosecutors from using illegally seized evidence, but *Wolf* permitted *state* prosecutors to do so.

Said Justice Clark, ". . . after its [*Wolf's*] dozen years on our books, [we] are led by it to close the only courtroom door remaining open to evidence secured by official lawlessness in flagrant abuse of that basic right, reserved to all persons as a specific guarantee against that very same unlawful conduct. We hold that all evidence obtained by search and seizure in violation of the Constitution is, by that same authority, inadmissible in a state court."

The authority Justice Clark referred to is the Fourth Amendment, which forbids illegal searches and seizures.

"There is no war between the Constitution and common sense," Justice Clark said. "Presently a federal prosecutor may make no use of evidence illegally seized, but a state's attorney across the street may, although he supposedly is operating under the enforcement prohibition of the same Amendment. Thus the state, by admitting evidence unlawfully seized, serves to encourage disobedience to the Federal Constitution which it is bound to uphold."

Justice Douglas concurred that Miss Mapp's conviction should be reversed, but because he felt Ohio's law under which she was convicted was unconstitutional. This was the point Miss Mapp's attorneys had argued. He ignored the search-and-seizure question.

The dissenters hammered the Court—as have many law-review articles—for making an important ruling on material that was not argued before the Court. The issue was the Ohio law, not the search and seizure. Why the Court ignored the issue and took up the point it did can only be guessed. Justice Clark and many others had disliked the *Wolf* decision since it was made. They saw in Miss Mapp's arrest a particularly flagrant abuse of police power. The Court may have thought it an appealing case by which to strike down such abuses.

Not only did the dissenters not like the Court's "reach" in *Mapp;* they also didn't like what they reached for. They disagreed that *Wolf* should be overruled, basing their contention on the argument that state courts should not be "federalized."

". . . The very fact on which the majority relies . . . points away from the need of replacing voluntary state action with Federal compulsion," said Justice Harlan in his dissent. "The preservation of a proper balance between state and federal responsibility in the actions of criminal justice demands patience on the part of those who might like to see things move faster among the states in this respect. Problems of criminal law enforcement vary widely from state to state. . . . For us the question remains, as it always has been, one of state powers, not one of passing judgment on the wisdom of one state course or another."

Mapp v. Ohio has been widely acclaimed as a landmark court decision extending the protection of the federal Constitution to all Americans. Since *Mapp,* a man's home and person have been protected more than ever before against unreasonable police searches.

Where *Mapp* has caused problems is when police searches have not been unreasonable. Suppose police know that bookmakers are maintaining an illegal gambling place in a certain house. Further suppose that police obtain a legal warrant to enter the house and search it for evidence. Must the police then knock on the door and announce that they are police? This is what all federal officers and some state authorities are required to do. The effect of this is often destruction of the evidence, for gamblers now use "flash paper" to take bets or to write numbers on, so named because it burns in a flash, destroying the evidence. Whether states can exempt officers from knocking in such cases has yet to be tested.

Or suppose a policeman sees a man lurking outside a store. He watches him and suspects he is about to break into the premises. He stops him and pats his clothing to see if he is armed—"frisking," as it is called. Is that an illegal search? If he finds a gun on him which the suspect is carrying in violation of state gun laws, was it illegally seized as evidence? Can it be used against him?

If the policeman frisks in the circumstances just described, most people would consider it a reasonable police action. If, however, the officer frisked people indiscriminately without good reason, that would be unreasonable. But where to draw the line? These questions, both reflected in legislation recently passed by the state of New York, have to be tested in the courts.

Suppose police stop a car for going through a red light and in the back seat they spot a box which turns out to contain stolen goods. Is that a legal search? Can the stolen goods be used in evidence? Or let's pose the problem of *Preston v. U.S.* (376 U.S. 364). In this case Preston was arrested for vagrancy while seated in an automobile. The car was not searched at the time of the arrest but was driven to a garage. Later, a thorough search without a warrant yielded two revolvers and other items usable in a robbery. Preston confessed and was indicted. The Supreme Court held that the search was illegal because it was not done at the time of the arrest.

It appears the search would have been legal had it been made immediately and if the officers had been looking for weapons which could have been used against them. In other words, it is legal to search without a warrant if done simultaneously with an arrest, for the purpose of protecting the officers from injury. Police are endeavoring to apply this "for my own protection" rule to frisks and many other searches conducted without warrants. That still does not answer the question of whether the evidence obtained in such protective searches can be used in court.

Since *Mapp*, another newly developed police practice has been to declare that the suspect dropped the evidence on the street. This means the officer did not have to make any search. More than one legal observer has contended that some police are committing perjury by claiming the suspect dropped the evidence when in fact he was searched.

The Supreme Court keeps picking its way through this search-and-seizure swamp opened by *Mapp*. In 1965 it declared that *Mapp* was not retroactive—that is, persons convicted on the basis of illegally seized evidence could not be freed, nor could they ask for new trials. In other recent cases, notably *Aguilar v. Texas* (378 U.S. 108), the Court has moved to require police seeking search warrants in state courts to provide more evidence of the need to conduct the search. In the past, officers simply referred to unsupported "tips" or suspicions when asking a judge for a warrant. Now the Court says the officers must provide enough facts on which the judge can make an independent, nonpartisan decision on the need for the warrant.

Another major area where the Supreme Court has been moving to protect individual rights, at the expense of long-standing police and prosecution practices, is in the matter of self-incrimination. The Fifth Amendment says "no person . . . shall be compelled in any criminal case to be a witness against himself. . . ." This is the famed phrase referred to in the expression "taking the Fifth" to avoid answering questions.

Perhaps no aspect of American civil liberties has been used or challenged more. Men of learning, thoughtfulness and humanity have suggested the Constitution be amended to remove this privilege of silence, contending it is used by subversives, criminals and assorted lawbreakers, while the honest, law-abiding, patriotic citizen seldom, if ever, has need of it. And it is true that the nature of law is such that the innocent man wants to talk, the more the better, while the guilty person wants silence.

Yet only the most optimistic can believe that this great citadel of liberty will be taken away. The problem is how to use it—and not abuse it. And this is a problem left largely to the courts.

In the late 1940s and early 1950s the Court gave wide latitude to those forces seeking to compel self-incrimination. Congressional committees investigating Communist influences in American life impaled witness after witness on the spike of publicity and compelled them to testify. If they refused, they were held in contempt of Congress and jailed. If they talked, they were prosecuted as Communists or perjurers. This practice was justified on the basis of protecting national security, and many Court decisions upheld this view. Consistently in the minority were Justices Black and Douglas, those judicial fortresses of individual liberty.

"Public opinion being what it now is," wrote Justice Black in a memorable dissent, "few will protest the conviction of these Communist petitioners. There is hope, however, that in calmer times, when present pressures, passions and fears subside, this or some later Court will restore the First Amendment liberties to the high preferred place where they belong in a free society." And in another dissent he said, "Our Constitution assumes the common sense of the people and their attachment to our country will enable them, after free discussion, to withstand ideas that are wrong. To say that our patriotism must be protected against false ideas by means other than these is, I think, to make a baseless charge."

Much has been written praising Black and Douglas and criticizing the Vinson Court for failure to thwart the inquisitional hearings conducted by the House Un-American Activities Committee and by the Senate Committee under the late Senator Joseph R. McCarthy of Wisconsin. These hearings were often "witch hunts," conducted amid great publicity, wherein "defendants," many of high reputation and position, were accused of Communist or "fellow traveling" opinions. The "witnesses" before the committee were given no proper opportunity to reply to the charges or to cross-examine those testifying against them or to call witnesses on their own behalf. Nor could they reply to charges made on the Senate or House floor or even sue the Senator or Representative who uttered them, for Congressmen are immune from libel laws when speaking on the floor of Congress.

When the careful, dispassionate history of this era is written, it may be held that the Vinson Court could have curbed these Congressional committees by more courageous decisions in favor of individual rights. Yet the histories will have to note that the "dominant opinion" of the time was a hysterical pursuit of ideological conformity. Dissent, nonconformity in politics, economic theory or religion were held in low esteem, if tolerated at all.

This dampening of the fires of liberty did not last, and when the Warren Court began to strike down convictions for contempt of Congress, perjury before Congressional committees and for membership in subversive organizations, the Court was clearly on the side of dominant opinion once again.

Congress had its own ideas, though. Abusive critics found the Court—usually Chief Justice Warren—believers in Communism. Legislation was introduced to curb the Court's right of review, but it died aborning, proof the Court had correctly estimated public feeling. The criticisms made of the Court in the middle and late 1950s are among the most heated ever made, as those listed in the opening chapter indicate. Yet it must be said that less than a decade later the Congressional hearings, the Court decisions and the criticisms by Congressmen of the Court have rapidly receded in importance. No great contribution to law was made one way or the other, and it is suspected that all the fuss has been over what will eventually be a footnote in history.

Where history is being made is in the extension of the Fifth Amendment privilege against self-incrimination to criminal law. An important case involved William Malloy of Windsor, Connecticut, who was convicted of a minor betting charge in Hartford in 1959. He was sentenced to ninety days in jail and fined $50.

In 1961 Malloy was called before the inquiry into gambling and other illegal practices in Hartford. He was asked questions about his 1959 arrest and about whether he knew certain individuals. Malloy refused to answer, taking the Fifth Amendment. The investigative body told him he was immune from further prosecution, but he persisted in taking the Fifth—and he gave no explanation of how he believed his testimony might incriminate him.

The Connecticut Supreme Court of Errors found that Malloy had not properly invoked his privilege. It ruled that the mere assertion that he might be incriminated without giving some reason was not enough to avoid answering apparently innocent questions. The Connecticut tribunal also took note that the Fifth Amendment to the federal Constitution did not apply to the states. The Supreme Court had so ruled in 1908, an opinion which was upheld in 1947, although by only a 5–4 vote.

In 1964 the Supreme Court held that Malloy did not have to testify, thus overruling its historic earlier decisions. Justice Brennan, joined by Chief Justice Warren and Justices Black, Douglas and Goldberg, ruled that the Fifth Amendment applies to the states as well as to the federal government. Justices Harlan, White and Stewart objected on the ground that the ruling undermined the federal system and compelled uniformity.

On the same day the Court, by a 6–3 vote in *Murphy v. Waterfront Commission* (378 U.S. 52), reversed earlier decisions dealing with self-incrimination in different jurisdictions. In this case Murphy had refused to testify to the Waterfront Commission of New York about some labor matters in Hoboken, New Jersey, on the ground that, although the commission granted him immunity from charges, he would be liable to a federal prosecution. And he was right, for at that time federal and state agencies could whipsaw a witness, compelling him to testify in a state inquiry, while leaving him open to charges in federal court. The decision, written by Justice Goldberg, prohibited this practice.

Closely related to this case is the matter of double jeopardy. The Constitution guarantees that no American can be tried twice for the same crime. Yet men are, regularly. One of the oddities of the federal system is that a man who robs a bank can be tried in federal courts for bank robbery and in state courts for armed robbery. If he kills someone in the robbery, he can be tried for bank robbery in the federal courts, murder in the state.

To say this is not double jeopardy is to raise a technicality. He is not tried twice in the same jurisdiction. It is a case of successive prosecutions—semantics of scant comfort to a defendant.

At this writing successive prosecutions are constitutional, but this issue seems likely to come before the Court.

Most of the public reaction to the major Supreme Court decisions has been on those dealing with segregation, school prayer and equal representation. Relatively little has been written and said about those recent landmark decisions in the field of the criminal-law enforcement. To be sure, police have been outraged. Public prosecutors have denounced the rulings. Lewis F. Powell, Jr., when president of the American Bar Association, said, "There are valid reasons for criminals to think that crime does pay and that slow and fumbling justice can be evaded. Society cannot await the millennium when the underlying causes of crime have been removed. We must act now."

Powell was referring to sharp increases in crime rates nationally and in most cities. The crime rate is increasing faster than the population. There is a serious crime every twenty-five seconds. Every three minutes someone is murdered, forcibly raped or assaulted with intent to kill. An American is murdered every hour, raped every thirty-two minutes. A robbery occurs every six minutes, a burglary every thirty-five seconds, a larceny of an amount over $50 every minute and an auto theft every ninety seconds. Crime costs $27 billion a year in this country. The "take" from illegal gambling is $50 billion and the profits to gamblers is $10 billion.

These are FBI figures, which are challenged by some who feel they are statistically improper, but this argument cannot hide the existence of a great deal of crime in the country, nor, worse, a growing feeling of lawlessness, that crime does somehow pay, that "unjust" laws don't need to be obeyed, that only the dumb and the unlucky get caught.

Thus we have the situation wherein recent Court decisions seem to have undermined long-standing police and prosecution practices at a time when the need for law enforcement is at its highest. The Court rulings and their effect on law enforcement have been aired by police, prosecutors, judges and the legal profession. But the general public seems less concerned.

It may be said that the public is generally ambivalent. People want police protection, yet they do not want to be arrested or bothered or curtailed by police activity. They want speeders arrested, but they do not want a radar trap which will catch them. They want traffic deaths lowered, but they do not want to pay for more policemen.

This conflict shows up again when the individual citizen is pleased to have police "slapped down" for an illegal search or unreasonable arrest, yet is disturbed when a known gangster or admitted murderer is freed because the evidence against him was improperly seized or his confession was made without a lawyer being present.

In this and the preceding chapter, we have tried to point up some of the questions concerning criminal procedures that will have to be resolved in years to come. Other problems will arise, keeping criminal-law enforcement in the forefront for many years.

It seems most likely, though, that the Court, in its decisions, is forcing a major overhaul of our institutions and practices of law enforcement. President Johnson has already appointed a top-level commission to recommend legislation. The Court has a functioning committee to examine judicial procedures in criminal law. A committee of the American Bar Association headed by Judge Edward Lumbard, chief judge of the U.S. Court of Appeals in New York, is drafting rules to update many antiquated areas of American criminal law. All of this may well produce results.

It is possible to guess—but no more than that—some changes that may eventually occur. There may be alterations in the practice of police interrogation. If police cannot question a man without his lawyer being present, some limitations must be placed on what that lawyer can do. The same applies to the role of both the prosecutor and the defense attorney at the trial.

The Court indicates that it will soon rule on the constitutionality of juvenile-court procedures wherein defendants do not receive the same safeguards afforded in adult courts; on alleged discrimination of application of rape laws to Negroes; on "deals" between trial judges, prosecutors and defense counsels wherein the defendant pleads guilty to a lesser offense to receive a lighter sentence. Indeed, the whole question of sentencing, wherein one defendant receives a more stringent penalty than another man committing a similar crime in another jurisdiction, seems likely to go before the Court.

We may be heading for a fundamental change in our whole adversary concept of justice, wherein each side of a criminal trial is antagonistic to the other and may the best man (or lawyer) win. The point of law can hardly be to convict innocent men or to free guilty ones. The point and the practice of the law must be to determine guilt and achieve justice. For many years the scales of justice tipped toward law enforcement. Now it seems to be tipping toward the lawless. Years to come should see a better balance.

A vital concern sure to be a Supreme Court issue of the future is that involved in the new investigative techniques. Police have at their fingertips electronic devices that can hear through walls, pick up one conversation in a stadium full of people, photograph in the dark, positively identify one man's voice from all other men's, listen in California to a conversation taking place in a locked, shuttered room in New York or any other town.

At the moment, use of these and many other techniques are illegal. Their use in criminal trials is severely limited. The use that can be made of these electronic and other scientific devices—both by police and by criminals—will have to be agreed upon. It makes little sense to permit criminals to use these techniques—legally or illegally —while denying their use to law enforcement. It would be like denying the use of cars and two-way radios to police, while permitting crooks to have them. The use of scientific advancements in law enforcement cannot and should not be denied.

As you have noticed, many of the Supreme Court decisions in the area of criminal-law enforcement have been close, 5–4 or 6–3. Some were even more divided than that. With several members of the Court reaching advanced age, future appointments will have a close bearing on future decisions in this difficult area.

Too, since dominant opinion is not well formed on these issues, it would seem the Court will have great power in shaping it.

XI. ENTERING THE
POLITICAL THICKET

> *We cannot believe it will make the old ship of state slip one knot for this Court to say that, in choosing their representatives, the people should have one vote for one man, as nearly as possible.*—Justice Hugo L. Black, orally from the bench, WESBERRY V. SANDERS

In the late 1950s Charles W. Baker and other residents of Tennessee went to court in what had to be the "lostest" of lost causes. They wanted the court to reapportion the state legislature. They were victims of unequal representation. Their votes didn't count as much as another man's living in another part of the state.

Just how unequal Tennessee's representation was had been figured out arithmetically. Tennessee's legislature consisted of a 33-member Senate and a 99-member House—and had since 1901. For almost threescore years Tennessee had governed itself by a system laid out when its population was 2,020,616 and it had 487,380 eligible voters. By 1960 Tennessee would have 3,567,087 residents and 2,092,891 eligible voters.

During the intervening years Tennessee had not only grown but its whole way of life had altered. The automobile, highways, airplanes, two world wars and industralization had turned Tennessee from a predominantly rural, farming area into a highly diversified

120

state with four large cities—Memphis, Knoxville, Nashville and Chattanooga—as well as many smaller cities, all with large sub-urban populations. The residents of these metropolitan areas now worked in factories and stores, not on farms. Their problems, needs, attitudes had changed.

But the legislature had not. The same 1901 districting remained. Moore County and Hamilton County each had the same number of representatives in the legislature, even though Hamilton County was now nineteen times larger than Moore County. The result was minority rule. Thirty-seven per cent of Tennessee's voters elected 20 of the 33 state senators and 40 per cent of the voters elected 63 of the 99 members of the lower house.

Similar inequities existed all over the state, the effect of which was to give representatives from rural counties almost total control over the legislative process. The combined block of rural representatives could easily outvote the combined urban-suburban representatives —and do it every time.

Between 1901 and 1960 many efforts were made to get Tennessee reapportioned. Representatives from cities and several governors tried to have the state redistricted to redress the balance away from rural representatives. All attempts failed, because votes of both houses of the state legislature were needed to change either the apportionment law or the state constitution. The dominating rural representatives were unwilling to have their political power cur-tailed in any way and consistently voted down any attempts to create election districts more nearly equal in population.

Tennessee's urban voters, such as Baker, tried numerous times to obtain relief through the courts, but the prevailing legal opinion as expressed by the Supreme Court was that legislative apportionment, no matter how unfair it might be, was a political and not a judicial question. In the words of Justice Frankfurter, reapportionment was a "political thicket" which the courts should not enter.

So urban voters such as Baker remained victims of unequal representation, victims without any practical way to improve their plight. All they could do, it seemed, was to grin and bear it, just as Tennessee urban voters had been doing for a half century.

If they wished, Baker and his friends might have taken comfort in the knowledge that they were no better and no worse off than city dwellers in most states. The unequal representation in Tennessee differed only in degree from that in nearly every state, for there existed a nationwide pattern of rural domination of legislatures.

Was this bad? Not really—until the Great Depression of 1929. Then the severe problems created by that economic disaster demonstrated that most (not all, certainly) small-town, rural politicians were too provincial, too conservative, too uninformed, too out of touch to cope with complex problems of poverty, unemployment, public-works projects, bank failures, strikes, relief and housing. Rural officeholders tended to be self-sufficient farmers and small shopkeepers unwilling to pay higher taxes to support public welfare and unemployment insurance for city dwellers who, not living on the land, had no utter chance to be self-sufficient in a time of great unemployment. Although equal representation may not have resulted in a different situation, the result in 1929 was impasse and inaction, into which the federal government moved with "New Deal" legislation, tackling the urban social and economic problems on a national level.

It was a trend never reversed. World War II intensified the national war effort. Postwar economic slumps, foreign-aid commitments, technological advances, the Cold War, space exploration and forced continuation of federal domination occurred. Strong, aggressive state legislatures could have moved more often to be aggressive in these problem areas—and sometimes they were. But rural domination continued to keep conservativeness a bargain and governmental inventiveness at a premium.

States' rights, so often defended by state politicians, all too often did not carry with it a sense of state responsibility. State representatives worried more about remaining in office and in control of the legislative process than they did about the public's desire for bold solutions to problems, though obviously rural domination need not imply lack of "governmental inventiveness."

Yet when Charles Baker asked the U.S. District Court for the Middle District of Tennessee for a declaration that Tennessee's apportionment act of 1901 was unconstitutional and sought an injunction restraining the state from conducting any further elections under the act, he was, it seemed, whistling past the judicial graveyard. The court had already ruled that reapportionment was a political thicket the courts should not enter. After all, for the courts to pass upon the quality of representation in a state legislature would be a gross interference in state politics by a federal court and massive meddling in the legislative branch of government. Separation of powers between the legislative, executive and judicial branches of government was a keystone of our democracy.

So it seemed that Baker's petition, no matter how justified one might think his contention was, had little chance in the courts. Yet a change was in the wind. John F. Kennedy, a young man of this century and this era, had been elected President, propelled into office on a promise of change and the opening of a New Frontier. Somehow, like a political alchemist, he played a part in renewing the nation's sense of destiny, its hope of accomplishment and improvement and its desire to rethink and to reshape old institutions and practices.

A three-judge district court dismissed Baker's action on the grounds that it lacked jurisdiction and that he had failed to show a claim for relief that could be granted. In other words, how could a court reapportion a legislature?

Baker v. Carr (369 U.S. 186) went to the Supreme Court. It was argued in 1960 and reargued in 1961. As Justice Clark pointed out in a concurring opinion, the case was held over for two years and argued for a total of six hours, three times the normal case.

Finally, on March 26, 1962, the high court, in one of the most historic of its decisions, ruled not in favor of Baker but simply that he had a point. Justice Brennan, speaking for a 6–3 majority, did not rule on the question of whether Tennessee's legislature was properly apportioned. All the Court said was that Baker, as a voter and taxpayer, had a right to bring court suit challenging the constitutionality of the state apportionment law and that the courts could decide the issue and order the legislature to be reapportioned, if they so wished. The Court thereby entered the political thicket.

Justice Brennan's opinion was highly legalistic, leaning heavily on history and precedents. His language was exceedingly careful and restrained. In the end the Court sent the case back to the district court for hearing on the issues Baker had raised—the fairness of Tennessee's apportionment.

Justice Clark's opinion, while it concurred with the majority, went a lot further. If he'd had his way, he would have decided right then that Tennessee's legislature was malapportioned. Said Justice Clark, ". . . no one, not even the state nor the dissenters, has come up with any rational basis for Tennessee's apportionment statute. . . . Certainly there must be some rational design to a state's districting. The discrimination here does not fit any pattern—as I have said, it is but a crazy quilt."

Justice Clark then seemed to express the unstated thinking of the majority: ". . . I would not consider intervention by this Court into so delicate a field if there were any other relief available to the people of Tennessee. But the majority of the people of Tennessee have no practical opportunity for exerting their political weight at the polls to correct the existing 'invidious discrimination.' Tennessee has no initiative and referendum. I have searched diligently for other 'practical opportunities' present under the law. I find none other than through the Federal Courts. The majority of the voters have been caught up in a legislative straitjacket. . . . Legislative policy has riveted the present seats in the Assembly to their respective constituencies and by the rates of their incumbents a reapportionment of any kind is prevented. The people have been rebuffed at the hands of the Assembly. They have tried the constitutional convention route, but since the call [for the convention] must originate in the Assembly, it, too, has been fruitless.

"They have tried Tennessee Courts with the same result, and the Governors have fought the tide only to flounder. It is said that there is recourse in Congress and perhaps that might be, but from a practical standpoint this is without substance. To date Congress has never undertaken such a task in any state. We, therefore, must conclude that the people of Tennessee are stymied and without judicial intervention will be saddled with the present discrimination in the affairs of their state government."

Thus Justice Clark and apparently the rest of the majority took a strongly activist position that an injustice was occurring and, all other recourses having failed, it was up to the federal courts to correct the injustice.

This activist role was a red flag before hard-charging Justices Frankfurter and Harlan. "Such a massive repudiation of the experience of our whole past in asserting destructively novel judicial power," wrote Justice Frankfurter in a stinging dissent, "demands . . . analysis of the role of this Court in our constitutional system."

Intervention in such a political question, he warned, "may well injure this Court's position as the ultimate organ of 'the supreme law of the land.' . . ." He said the "Court's authority—possessed of neither the pen nor the sword—ultimately rests on sustained public confidence and their moral sanction. Such feeling must be mounted by the Court's complete detachment in fact and in application from political entanglements and by abstention from injecting itself into the clash of . . . forces in political settlements. . . ."

Justice Harlan, also joined by Justice Frankfurter, said, "I can find nothing in the Equal Protection Clause [of the Fourteenth Amendment] or elsewhere in the Constitution which expressly or impliedly supports the view that state legislatures must be structured as to reflect with approximate equality the voice of every voter. . . ."

The deed was done. The Court had hung out a shingle saying it was hearing redistricting cases, and they arrived by the dozen. The following year, 1963, the Court, in *Gray v. Sanders* (373 U.S. 368), declared the unit vote system in primary elections to be unconstitutional. The case came from Georgia, one of only a few states using the system. In this, candidates for each political party's nomination for governor would not be elected at large. Each county or other subdivision would be assigned a certain number of unit votes, depending on size or population. Whoever got the most popular votes in each county got all the unit votes. The unit votes were heavily weighed in favor of rural counties, so that a candidate could get a majority of popular votes statewide but still lose out in the unit vote. In practical application, candidates ignored the heavily populated cities to campaign in the sparsely populated rural areas.

Then in February 1964 the Supreme Court rendered a decision which surprised the nation—and a few of its own members.

The case was brought by James P. Wesberry, Jr., and another man against Carl E. Sanders, then the Governor of Georgia. Wesberry was a voter in Georgia's Fifth Congressional District, which, in the 1960 census, had a population of 823,680, more than twice the population of the *average* congressional district in Georgia, the average being 394,312 residents. Wesberry and the other petitioner contended that this was a violation of their rights under the Consti-

tution and asked the Court to declare the Georgia law which established the congressional districts void and to prevent any more
members of the United States House of Representatives from being
elected under the act.

More facts were that Georgia's Fifth Congressional District consisted of DeKalb, Rockdale and Fulton counties. Georgia had nine
districts electing congressmen. The largest in size was the Fifth, the
smallest was the Ninth District with 272,154 population, less than
half as many as the Fifth. Thus the elected Representative from
Georgia's Fifth District represented two to three times as many
citizens as the Representative from the Ninth District. In fact, the
population of Fulton County alone, where Wesberry lived, exceeded
the entire Ninth District by 40 per cent.

Again the situation in Georgia was similar to that elsewhere
around the nation. Many political scientists attributed the recent
"decline" of the House as a legislative body—it seemed overly tied
to procedures and unable to pass forward-looking legislation—to the
large number of malapportioned districts. Just how bad the situation
was can be shown from the following table, showing the disparity
between the largest congressional district and the smallest in each
state:

STATE	LARGEST DISTRICT	SMALLEST DISTRICT
Alabama	*All representatives elected at large*	
Alaska	*Elected at large*	
Arizona	663,510	198,236
Arkansas	575,385	332,844
California	588,933	301,872
Colorado	653,954	195,551
Connecticut	689,555	318,942
Delaware	*Elected at large*	
Florida	660,345	237,235
Georgia	823,680	272,154
Hawaii	*Elected at large*	
Idaho	409,949	257,242
Illinois	552,582	278,703
Indiana	697,567	290,596
Iowa	442,406	353,156
Kansas	539,592	373,583

STATE	LARGEST DISTRICT	SMALLEST DISTRICT
Kentucky	610,947	350,838
Louisiana	536,029	262,850
Maine	505,465	463,800
Maryland	711,045	243,570
Massachusetts	478,376	376,336
Michigan	802,994	117,431
Minnesota	482,872	375,475
Mississippi	608,441	295,072
Missouri	506,854	378,499
Montana	400,573	274,194
Nebraska	530,507	404,695
Nevada	Elected at large	
New Hampshire	331,818	275,103
New Jersey	585,586	255,165
New Mexico	Elected at large	
New York	471,001	350,186
North Carolina	491,461	299,156
North Dakota	333,290	299,156
Ohio	724,156	235,288
Oklahoma	552,863	227,692
Oregon	522,813	265,164
Pennsylvania	553,154	303,026
Rhode Island	459,706	399,782
South Carolina	531,555	302,235
South Dakota	497,669	182,845
Tennessee	627,019	223,387
Texas	951,527	216,371
Utah	572,654	317,973
Vermont	Elected at large	
Virginia	539,618	312,890
Washington	510,512	342,540
West Virginia	422,046	303,098
Wisconsin	530,316	236,870
Wyoming	Elected at large	

A quick study of this lists shows only a handful of states, other than those electing Representatives at large, which are even approximately equal in size. On the other hand, in seventeen states the largest district is more than twice the size of the smallest. In Colorado, Maryland, Tennessee, South Dakota and Ohio the largest district is approximately three times as large as the smallest, and in

Michigan and Texas the disparity is four times. Clearly the record shows unequal representation.

Wesberry v. Sanders (376 U.S. 1) was decided February 17, 1964, with Justice Black writing the opinion for the majority, which included Chief Justice Warren and Justices Douglas, Brennan, White and Goldberg.

"We agree with the District Court that the 1931 Georgia Apportionment Act grossly discriminates against voters in the Fifth Congressional District . . ." said Justice Black—a bit of sarcasm, for the district court had dismissed Wesberry's claim as not one courts could decide. The high court was reversing the lower court.

"We hold that . . . Article 1, Section 2 [of the United States Constitution] . . . means that as nearly as practicable one man's vote in a Congressional election is to be worth as much as another's. This rule is followed automatically, of course, when Representatives are chosen as a group on a statewide basis, as was a widespread practice in the first 50 years of our nation's history. . . .

"To say that a vote is worth more in one district than in another would not only run counter to our fundamental ideas of democratic government, it would cast aside the principle of a House of Representatives elected 'by the people,' a principle tenaciously fought for and established at the Constitutional Convention." Justice Black then presented an extensive review of the "Great Compromise" at the Constitutional Convention at which it was decided the Senate should reflect states and the House population. ". . . when the delegates agreed that the House should represent 'people,'" said the Justice, "they intended that in allocating Congressmen, the number assigned to each state should be determined solely by the number of the state's inhabitants."

Justice Black concluded, "while it may not be possible to derive Congressional districts with mathematical precision, that is no excuse for ignoring our Constitution's plain objective of making equal representation for equal numbers of people the fundamental goal for the House of Representatives. That is the high standard of justice and common sense which the Founders set for us."

The words were hardly spoken when they launched a legal and historical argument that will probably never be settled: Whether he and the majority were correct in deciding the issue on Article 1, Section 2, which reads, "The House of Representatives shall be composed of members chosen every second year by the people of the several states. . . . "

Justice Black endeavored to show historically that the words "by the people" meant a rule of "one person, one vote." Justice Harlan, in a memorable dissent, gave his own view of history which produced the opposite result, then tossed Sections 4 and 5 of Article 1 at the majority.

Section 4 reads: "The times, places and manner of holding elections for Senators and Representatives shall be prescribed in each state by the legislature thereof; but the Congress may at any time by law make or alter such regulations, except as to the places of choosing Senators."

Section 5: "Each house shall be the judge of the elections, returns and qualifications of its own members. . . ."

Justice Harlan maintained in biting language that the Constitution said the state legislatures and Congress prescribed the manner of elections and that the judiciary had no business interfering.

There can be little doubt that if the nation's law professors and constitutional authorities were polled at this time, they would endorse Justice Harlan's view of history. This is the stuff of historical controversy, but to the man in the street it is a case of how many angels can fit on the head of a pin. The result is the same.

Justice Clark, while hardly a friend to malapportionment, could not buy the majority's interpretation. He felt the issue should have been decided on the basis of the equal-protection clause of the Fourteenth Amendment and voted to send the case back to the district court for argument on this issue.

Justice Harlan liked neither the logic nor the result. In his caustic dissent, in which Justice Stewart largely joined, he blistered his colleagues: "I had not expected to witness the day when the Supreme Court of the United States would make a decision which casts grave doubt on the Constitutionality of the composition of the House of Representatives."

Justice Harlan said the ruling "impugns the validity of the election of 398 Representatives from 37 states, leaving a 'Constitutional' House of 37 members. . . ." He contended that the Court, in effect, had called a coordinate branch of the federal government unconstitutional and predicted "extraordinary consequences" of the act.

The statement by Justice Harlan was so damaging that Justice

Black, replying to him orally from the bench, said, "It is said some-how that we are holding the whole Congress unconstitutional. We do not look at the future with such dark glasses. We cannot believe it will make the old ship of state slip one knot for this Court to say that, in choosing their Representatives, the people should have one vote for one man, as nearly as possible."

Justice Harlan had a few more choice words reserved for his dissent. "The unstated premise of the Court's conclusion quite obviously is that the Congress had not dealt and the Court believes it will not deal with the problem of Congressional reapportionment in accordance with what the Court believes to be sound political principles. . . . This Court . . . is not simply undertaking to exercise a power which the Constitution reserved to Congress; it is also overruling a Congressional judgment." The Justice maintained that Congress had considered reapportionment and deliberately refused to pass legislation to require it.

"The claim for judicial relief in this case, " continued Justice Harlan, "strikes at one of our fundamental doctrines of our system of government, the separation of powers. . . . The Constitution does not confer on the Court blanket authority to step into every situation where the political branch may be thought to have fallen short. . . .

"What is done today saps the political process. The process of judicial intervention in matters of this sort cannot but encourage popular inertia in efforts for political reform through the political process, with the inevitable result that the process is itself weakened. By yielding to the demand for a judicial remedy in this instance, the Court, in my view, does a disservice, both to itself and to the broader values of our system of government."

Thus, by February 1964 the battle lines had been drawn between judicial activism and judicial restraint, between judicial reform and political reform. It was legislative perogative versus judicial power. That which Baker and his associates had started in Tennessee years before had spread to include the unit-vote system in state primaries and the apportionment of the House of Representatives.

Yet that which had been originally sought—the reapportionment of state legislatures—had not yet been ruled upon. The day would soon come—and surprise nearly everyone.

XII. ONE MAN, ONE VOTE

Legislatures represent people, not trees or acres.—Chief Justice Earl Warren for the Court in REYNOLDS V. SIMS—

This Court is not a panacea for every blot upon the public welfare . . . —Justice John Marshall Harlan, dissenting in REYNOLDS V. SIMS

After the Supreme Court entered the political thicket in *Baker v. Carr*, it was caught on briers from a dozen prickly state-apportionment cases. The issues were first battled in lower federal and state courts, but the guidelines set down by *Baker v. Carr* were not very taut. Lower-court judges did the best they could, but the result was confusion which only the Supreme Court could straighten out.

For example, how equal should legislative districts be in population? Could factors other than population—such as area, economic interests, race, ethnic origins—be considered in districting? Were both legislative houses to be reapportioned? How far should the courts go to force reapportionment?

Lower-court judges wrestled with these problems and came up with different answers. The perplexing result headed for the Court in a dozen cases.

Among these was one brought by B. A. Reynolds and other taxpayers of Jefferson County, Alabama, wherein lies Birmingham, the largest city. Reynolds had challenged the validity of the existing Alabama legislature, which consisted of a 35-member state senate elected from 35 districts varying in population from 15,417 to 634,864 and a 106-member house of representatives with a population-representation variance from 6,731 to 104,767. All of this was in accordance with the 1901 Alabama constitution.

Reynolds and the other plaintiffs asked the federal district court to reapportion the Alabama legislature provisionally, so that the rural political power could be diluted enough to allow the legislature to reapportion itself.

Faced with the prospects of court-ordered reapportionment, the Alabama legislature met in extraordinary session on July 12, 1962, and, in a hectic session, passed two reapportionment bills. The first proposed a state constitutional amendment creating a 67-man senate with one senator from each county, the counties varying in population from 10,726 to 634,864 (Jefferson County) and a 106-man house with population varying from 10,726 to 42,303. What was done was to give each of the 67 counties one seat in the house, then apportion the remaining 39 seats on the basis of population. Jefferson County with 634,864 population got seven additional members and Mobile County with 314,301 population received three.

The district court considered this plan on July 21 and ruled the senate plan "discriminatory, arbitrary and irrational." It didn't like the plan for the house much better but termed it a "step in the right direction, but an extremely short step."

The second or "standby" plan offered by the Alabama legislature would create a 35-member state senate elected from 35 senatorial districts varying in population from 31,175 to 634,864 and a 106-member house with population varying from 20,000 to over 52,000.

The court considered this plan, too, and was far from pleased, but it ordered the November 1962 elections held so as to elect the senate under the standby plan and the house under the "67-senator" plan. This legislature would sit provisionally to develop an effective plan for reapportionment. The elections were held, but no apportionment plan was forthcoming in 1963 or 1964.

The question of whether the three-judge district court had acted properly came before the Supreme Court November 13, 1963, and was decided June 15, 1964. The majority was 6–3 and the opinion was by Chief Justice Warren—in itself significant, for the Chief Justice normally reserves for himself those onerous tasks likely to draw the most controversy.

"Undeniably the Constitution of the United States protects the right of all qualified citizens to vote, in state as well as in Federal elections," said the Chief Justice. "The right to vote freely for the candidate of one's choice is the essence of a democratic society, and any restriction on that right strikes at the heart of representative government. The right of suffrage can be denied by a debasement or dilution of the weight of a citizen's vote just as effectually as by wholly prohibiting them from exercise of their franchise."

Then came one of the great moments of the law as the Chief Justice of the United States intoned these words: "Legislatures represent people, not trees or acres. Legislatures are elected by votes, not farms or cities or economic interests. As long as ours is a representative form of government and our legislatures are those instruments of government elected directly by and directly representative of the people, the right to elect legislatures in a free and unimpaired fashion is a bedrock of our political system.

"If a state statute provided that the votes of citizens in one part of a state should be given two times or five times or ten times the weight of votes of citizens in another part of the state, it could hardly be contended that the right to vote of those residing in the disfavored areas had not been effectively diluted. It would appear extraordinary to suggest that a state could be constitutionally permitted to pass a law providing that certain of the state's voters could vote two, five or ten times for the legislative representatives, while voters living elsewhere could vote only once. And it is inconceivable that a state law to the effect that in county votes for legislatures the votes of citizens in one part of the state would be multiplied by two, five or ten, while the votes of persons in another area would be counted only at face value, could be constitutionally sustained."

Again the Chief Justice drummed in his argument, "Logically, in a society ostensibly grounded on representative government, it would seem reasonable that a majority of the people of a state could elect a majority of the state's legislators. To conclude differently and to sanction minority control of the state legislature would appear to deny majority rights in a way that far surpasses any possible denial of minority rights that might otherwise be thought to result."

Chief Justice Warren then showed that he had read the comments of his colleagues and the nation's press: "We are told that the matter of apportionment in a state legislature is a complex and many-faceted one. We are advised that states can rationally consider factors other than population in apportioning legislative representation. We are admonished not to restrict the power of the state voters to impose different views as to political philosophy on their citizens. We are cautioned about the dangers of entering into political thickets and mathematical quagmires. Our answer is this: a denial of constitutionally-protected rights demands judicial protection; our oath and our office requires no less of us. . . .

"To the extent that a citizen's right to vote is debased, he is that much less a citizen. . . . A citizen, a qualified voter, is no more, nor no less so because he lives in the city or on a farm."

Then the majority delivered the "shocker." The Justices ruled that both houses of a bicameral legislature—that is, the state senate as well as the lower state house—must be apportioned on the basis of population. Most people had expected that area of geography would be allowed as a basis for upper-house apportionment. After all, isn't the United States Senate apportioned on the basis of two members from each state rather than on the population or area of the state? Shouldn't states be allowed to do the same, giving like numbers of representatives to their counties or other subdivisions?

This argument was rejected *en toto* by the Court. "Attempted reliance on the federal analogy," said the Chief Justice, "appears often to be little more than an after-the-fact rationalization in defense of maladjusted state apportionment arrangements." He pointed out that the original constitutions of thirty-six states provided that representation in both houses of the state legislature be based on population.

The Chief Justice noted, too, that the federal Congress was worked out as a great compromise between sovereign states, then added, "Political subdivisions of states—counties, cities or whatever—never were and never have been considered sovereign entities. They are only sub-governmental instrumentalities of the state."

Then he said that if only one house of legislatures were reapportioned, "The people might be almost as effectively thwarted as if neither house were apportioned on a population basis. . . . In all too many cases the problematical result would be frustration of the majority will through minority veto in the house not apportioned on a population basis."

The final blows to the political *status quo* in most states were ruling that the state could take geographic factors into consideration in apportioning, but not in such a way as to cause great disparity in population of the districts. Finally, the whole matter of apportionment was held to be a question of judicial review, and the courts were to take an active hand in effecting speedy reapportionment. The long delays in bringing about school desegregation were not to occur again.

Decisions were made in five other apportionment cases that day, with Chief Justice Warren writing the Court opinions in each case. The majorities varied slightly, but 6–3 was the dominant one. Attempts to reapportion New York, Virginia, Maryland, Delaware and Colorado were ruled unconstitutional for various reasons. Clearly, the Court was insisting that population be the dominant factor in the apportionment of both houses of state legislatures.

Most far reaching of these decisions was the one from Colorado, where a majority of the voters had approved a "little federal" plan, making the house roughly equal in population but allowing 33 per cent of the people to elect a senate majority. This was declared void by the Court, with Chief Justice Warren saying, "A citizen's constitutional rights can hardly be infringed simply because a majority of the people choose to do so."

Those Justices who disagreed with the majority could not agree in their views. Justice Clark, who had written the strong concurring opinion in *Baker v. Carr*, did not like the rule that both houses must be based on population. He felt one house could reflect area or some other factor. Justice Stewart agreed with some of the majority decisions, but on narrower grounds. He clearly was not in total agreement with the insistence on population alone.

Consistent with his earlier views, Justice Harlan dissented entirely. His words were at times acid, almost acrimonious. "The Court's elaboration of its new 'constitutional' doctrine indicates how far—and how unwisely—it has strayed from the appropriate bounds of its authority. The consequences of today's decision is that . . . the District Courts or, it may be, the state courts, are given blanket authority and the Constitutional duty to supervise apportionment of the state legislatures. It is difficult to imagine a more intolerable and insupportable interference by the Judiciary with the independent legislatures of the states."

He said the case "presents a jarring picture of courts threatening to take action in an area where they have no business entering, inevitably on the basis of political judgments which they are incompetent to make. They show legislatures of the states meeting in haste and deliberating and deciding in haste to avoid the threat of judicial interference."

Justice Harlan then listed ten factors which the Court had eliminated from consideration in reapportionment. They were (1) history; (2) "economic and other sorts of group interests"; (3) areas; (4) geographic considerations; (5) a desire "to insure effective representation for sparsely settled areas"; (6) "availability of access of citizens to their representatives"; (7) "theories of bicameralism (except those approved by this Court)"—his parentheses; (8) occupation; (9) "an attempt to balance urban and rural power"; and (10) the preference of a majority of voters in the state.

Observed Justice Harlan, "The only factor, other than population, seems to be political subdivisions, and it is unconstitutional if 'population is submerged as the controlling consideration.'"

The dissenter then referred to Chief Justice Warren's statement that legislators are elected by people and not by trees. "All this may be conceded," he said, "but it is surely equally obvious and in the context of elections more meaningful to note that people are not ciphers and that legislatures can represent their electors only by speaking for the interests—economic, social, political—many of which do not reflect the place where the electors live."

Justice Harlan said, "What is done today deepens my conviction that judicial entry into this realm is profoundly ill advised and constitutionally impermissible." The decision "cuts deeply into the fabric of our federalism," he said.

"Finally, these decisions give support to a current mistaken view of this Court and the constitutional function of this Court. This view, in a nutshell, is that every major social ill in the country can find its cure in some constitutional 'principle' and that this Court should 'take the lead' in promoting reform when other branches of government fail to act.

"This Court is not a panacea for every blot upon the public welfare, nor should this Court, ordained as a judicial body, be thought of as a general haven for reform movements. . . . This Court . . . does not serve its high purpose when it exceeds its authority, even to satisfy justified impatience with the slow workings of the political process."

In the short time since the Court made its reapportionment decisions, it has become possible to make some limited judgments on their effect. There is no doubt that the Court entered a political thicket. In state after state the federal and state courts are deeply involved in reapportionment, redistricting and litigation challenging the propriety and legality of legislative and judicial actions in this area. Courts have ordered special elections to be held, ordered congressmen and legislators to be elected at large, ordered new legislation to be drawn up, ordered new district lines to be mapped, ordered constitutional conventions to be convened, and, in general, have caused great distress and political upheaval among legislators and professional politicians.

The reapportionment process and the legal testing of it will continue for years. The Supreme Court will be hearing cases relative to this issue for many terms to come. It will surely have to decide if city councils, county boards of commissioners, school boards and other local governing units must also reapportion. The political thicket will doubtless extend through all aspects of government.

The effect may well be immeasurable. For many decades the country has lived under malapportionment. During those years the dominant voice in state and local politics has been—with many, many exceptions—the so-called "WASP"—that is, white Anglo-Saxon Protestant—living on farms and in small towns and cities. This remained significantly true during twenty years of Democratic control of the White House under Presidents Franklin D. Roosevelt and Harry S Truman. From 1932 to 1952 Democrats controlled the federal government largely because they consistently won by large majorities in most large cities. In 1960 John F. Kennedy used the large city vote to win the White House and so did Lyndon B. Johnson in 1964. On the national scene, with the exception of the personal victories won by Dwight D. Eisenhower in 1952 and 1956, the rural small-town WASP vote, the traditional pre-1930 strength of the Republican Party, has not even approached majority strength nationwide.

Even in state and local politics the rural vote has had to rely upon malapportionment to maintain control. In the Deep South, where conservatism is strongest, these views have been enhanced by malapportionment which deliberately disenfranchised the Negro and diluted the voting strength of urban and industrial residents.

The Supreme Court has swept all this away. The result, almost without doubt, will be dominance by the urban and suburban voter. Large minorities, such as Negroes, Jews, Catholics, Mexicans, Puerto Ricans, Italians, labor, college-educated, etc., will be able—if they vote as blocs—to elect a number of legislators commensurate with their voting strength. For the first time, representatives of urban minorities will begin to play significant roles in the legislative process.

The near future may well see the election of Negro mayors and other officeholders in large cities. City councils and state legislatures, North and South, could then become truly "integrated." Legislatures might begin to pass laws directly affecting the long-neglected problems of urban, suburban voters, some of which will be "novel" and supply plenty of fodder for the Supreme Court's judicial-review silo.

The results may be ragged and uneven, mistakes may be made and excesses may occur, but the nation surely will begin at the municipal and state level to solve the difficult social, economic, technological, financial and moral problems plaguing our great urban societies. Surely the result must be a lessening of domination by the federal government and more "grass roots" solutions to local problems. The growth of federal power at the expense of states' rights may find itself curbed as a result of the Supreme Court's reapportionment decisions.

At least, all this is a possible indication of the Court's ruling. Whether it is fulfilled, history will reveal.

In the short time since the decisions it is possible to say that for all the turmoil among politicians and all the newspaper headlines about new elections and legislative stalemates over reapportionment, the country has entered the political thicket rather calmly. Without doubt few Supreme Court decisions ever had such overwhelming support of a majority of the voters, for it was the majority which was underrepresented. The men in the Marble Palace did not have to give a second thought to where the dominant opinion lay.

Support for the high purpose of the Court's decision was overwhelming. Even Justice Harlan and those who wished the Court had not made the decision did not quarrel with the need to have reapportionment take place. They merely wished Congress or the legislatures had done it, not the courts.

The arguments raised against reapportionment are, to many, so illogical and intemperate as to be hardly worth mentioning in a serious review of the situation. The big fear is that the vote generated in cities is somehow tainted. City officeholders are thought to be more political, more "boss controlled" and less tolerant of minority rights, of regional differences, of economic needs of nonurban areas than the farmer-legislators were. There is no basis, these people say, other than pure unreasoning emotionalism to believe this, nor can it be assumed that farmers and rural citizens won't be represented in legislatures. They simply are less apt to dominate, which does not mean they will not be present to deliberate on laws. Since most legislative bodies work on a seniority system, strong-willed, able individual legislators, regardless of where they are elected from, will no doubt continue to wield great influence in legislatures.

Another major fear is that rural legislators will be dwarfed in number by a huge bloc of urban and suburban legislators. The likelihood of an urban-suburban bloc is small. Actually, the needs of city and suburbia differ. The conflicting attitudes of urban and suburban legislators may well be the great division in the legislatures of the future.

Whatever the future, one must today stand in awe of the stand taken by Justice Harlan. He had a point and he made it most effectively. As he said, "people are not ciphers" and the Court is "not a panacea for every blot upon the public welfare. . . . "

Justice Harlan objected not to the reapportionment but to the Court's doing it. Probably every other member of the Court would have wished the legislatures had done it themselves so the Court did not have to enter the thicket. Justice Harlan's dissent in favor of judicial restraint, coming in the tradition of Justice Frankfurter, may well stand for many years as a toll station to those who would use the courts as a roadway to utopia.

It seems that always in our history this nation has had the "voice in the wilderness," the individual with courage to warn of possible dangers in majority viewpoints. Many times he has been influential in changing the course and sometimes his view has become law. Justice Harlan performed this role admirably in the reapportionment cases.

XIII. OBSCENITY, PRIVACY AND OTHER PUZZLES

The Court welcomes you.—Chief Justice Earl Warren from the bench to Thurgood Marshall

In mid-October 1965 a tall, beefy man donned a set of striped pants, black vest and swallow-tailed morning coat and remarked to his amused seven- and nine-year-old sons, "Now isn't this the silliest get-up in the world?"

A few minutes later, standing beside United States Attorney General Nicholas deB. Katzenbach, he was introduced to the Justices of the Supreme Court as the 33rd U.S. Solicitor General. Chief Justice Warren beamed at the newcomer and, true to the formality of the occasion, intoned, "The Court welcomes you."

The man in the formal clothes and the new job was a familiar face, Thurgood Marshall. President Johnson had persuaded him to give up a lifelong sinecure as judge of the Court of Appeals to take the $28,500 a year post as Solicitor General, the third-ranking position in the Department of Justice. The Attorney General and his deputy outrank him.

At the time of his appointment, speculation was common that Marshall would eventually be named to the Supreme Court, making him the first Negro Justice in history.

Whether "Mr. Civil Rights" and ex-judge Thurgood Marshall

becomes Mr. Justice Marshall or not, he will in his new capacity
have great opportunity to shape justice during his period as Solicitor
General.

The Solicitor General is the government's attorney before the
Court. If any federal agency becomes involved in litigation on any
subject and appeals the case to the Supreme Court, it is the Solicitor
General who pleads the case. He prepares the briefs submitted to
the Court and makes the oral arguments. If it is a matter to which
the government is not a litigant but in which the government has an
interest—the school-segregation cases would be a good example—
the Solicitor General appears as a "friend of the court" (*amicus
curiae*) to make known the government's viewpoint.

The Solicitor General is a unique individual in the government.
He is a member of the executive branch of the government, yet the
Supreme Court expects him to be beyond partisanship. He is
expected to screen all the government appeals, bringing to the Court
only those cases of importance and high constitutional principle.
Furthermore, if the government is wrong in its appeal or argument,
the Solicitor General is expected to say so by "confessing error." In
short, the Solicitor General is expected to put the law, truth and
justice ahead of victory—a demand not made of many lawyers in
this country.

Because the government has had a succession of Solicitors General who performed their difficult tasks extraordinarily well, the
Supreme Court now hears about 66 per cent of the government's
petitions, compared with fewer than 10 per cent of those from
private lawyers.

The effect is to give the Solicitor General, Thurgood Marshall,
great power in shaping the issues which come before the Court. It is
known that Marshall is a civil libertarian in the traditions of Black,
Douglas and Warren, on civil rights and criminal procedures. His
attitudes toward other aspects of the law are less well known.

But certainly the nation has an able, shrewd, experienced and
honorable man as its chief advocate before the Court. The issues
discussed in this book, the great unanswered questions about life
and the law, some of which have been posed in these pages, will be
pleaded and argued—and thereby shaped—by Thurgood Marshall.

In this book we have examined school segregation, racial discrimination, criminal procedures, religious freedom and reapportionment as the great issues of our times.

Great they are, but they are far from the only issues. One of the most difficult to come before the Court involves censorship of obscene books, magazines and motion pictures—rather, how to define what is obscene. The Court has held since 1957 that obscenity may be prohibited by law but has not been able to agree on what is beyond the pale of the law.

Great confusion exists. On one hand there are those who have a rather restricted view of what is obscene. They believe it is dangerous and inciting to prurient interests to describe sexual activities in books, to publish still or motion pictures of such activities or even to portray them in an appealing way outside of marriage. The advocates of censorship—in general those interested in religion, morality and education—believe the virtually unrestricted publication of lurid magazines and sensational movies seduces young people with fraudulent ideas about sex and incites the depraved. They see increases in the number of criminal sex offenders as evidence of the need for censorship.

At the other extreme are the views of men such as Justices Black and Douglas that as regrettable and distasteful as such publications and productions are, they are protected under the First Amendment, which says, "Congress shall make no law . . . abridging the freedom of speech or of the press. . . ." To Justices Black and Douglas the words "shall make no law" mean just that: no law at all—none. Therefore, no governmental restriction can be made on anything written or said. No censorship at all should be permitted. The definition of obscenity is purely academic to them and not a matter for a legal concern. Only with unrestricted freedom can the common sense of the people reject that to which they individually object.

In between these two extremes are those who feel that society must impose some restriction to prohibit the obscene. In the numerous cases which have come before the Court dealing with obscenity and pornography, Justice Harlan has indicated his belief that "hardcore pornography" should be banned. The prevailing opinion of the Court is that obscenity is something "utterly without redeeming social importance." In general, it may be said that the Court, as of this writing, feels that obscene work, taken as a whole, must appeal to prurient interests.

As you can imagine, the "definition" demands definition. What is "prurient interest," "utterly without," "hard-core," "redeeming," "social" and "importance"? The Court has applied this rather elastic yardstick to a variety of movies and books which various persons have considered too objectionable for public consumption, but in most cases the Court has found some "redeeming social importance" or an absence of "hard-core pornography."

The result has been virtually no censorship of any kind and many legal actions to test the confusing definitions. It may be that obscenity is indefinable in a society such as ours, and judges will be asked to make their own, personal measurements of these factors.

A new approach to the problem originated in the Court on March 21, 1966, when it ruled 5–4 to uphold publisher Ralph Ginzberg's $28,000 fine and five-year federal sentence for selling the now defunct magazine *Eros* and two other publications through the United States mails. The decision created a new obscenity standard. It looked not at the content of the publication but the use made of it. Justice Brennan said Ginzberg's advertising of his publications was "titillating" and permeated with "the leer of the sensualist" so that he was in "the sordid business of pandering." The new rule for judging obscenity is this: "Where the purveyor's sole emphasis is on the sexually provocative aspects of his publications, that fact may be decisive in the determination of obscenity."

The opinion was greeted with praise and criticism as befits the controversy over censorship, but the moderate view was that the Court had, by judging the use made of a publication rather than its content, plowed new ground that at least offered a chance for more factual decisions in these difficult cases. Many problems remain, however, and the obscenity question seems certain to be one of the thorniest before the Court for many years.

A related constitutional issue involves freedom of the press. No newspaper, magazine or book publisher can print, nor an author write, that which damages the reputation of another or accuses him of a crime—unless he can prove that what he printed or said over the radio or television was the truth. As you can imagine, the question of what is the *true* "truth" is constantly being taken to court.

In recent years the number of libel and slander suits against publications and authors has gone up sharply, perhaps because individuals have been encouraged by some sensational, multimillion-dollar awards made by juries to injured parties.

The most recent rulings in this area seem to indicate that a publication may say just about anything it wishes about a public official as long as it does so without malice, but these are issues far from settled. For many years the country's press has been restricted in its freedom to print the truth not so much by the laws of libel but by the threat of a libel suit, the defense of which can be expensive. It would seem likely that the Court will move to defend the press against unjust suits and to give them wide latitude to comment freely on public affairs.

At the same time the press is being put under severe restrictions in the publication of news about criminal trials. The spectacle of scores of scrambling newspapermen and photographers "covering" the assassination of President Kennedy shocked the nation and led to a demand for reforms, to prevent the spectacle and to insure a fair trial for the defendants. In an important recent case, the Court upset the 1954 conviction of Dr. Samuel H. Sheppard, Cleveland, Ohio, osteopath, on the ground that "virulent publicity" created "trial by newspaper" and prevented him from receiving a fair trial.

Considerable wordage and printers' ink has gone into discussion of the individual's "right to privacy." The Constitution does not use the term, but many experts believe the right to be let alone is implied in the Constitutional guarantees affecting speech, religion, searches and seizures, self-incrimination.

In 1965 the Court, by a 7–2 vote, struck down Connecticut's 1879 law banning dissemination of information about birth control. In his majority opinion Justice Douglas said, "We deal with a right of privacy older than the Bill of Rights—older than our political parties, older than our school system. Marriage is a coming together for better or for worse, hopefully enduring, and intimate to a degree of being sacred. The association promotes a way of life, not causes;

a harmony in living, not political faith; a bilateral loyalty, not commercial or social projects. Yet, it is an association for as noble a purpose as any involved in our prior decisions."

Justice Douglas spoke of the "zone of privacy" created by the First, Third, Fourth, Fifth, Ninth and Fourteenth Amendments.

Other members of the majority, while concurring in the result, were widely divided over what portion of the Constitution made Connecticut's law void. But Justice Douglas certainly created a precedent involving the "right to privacy."

Much more will be heard about this in years to come. The right to privacy, if it exists legally, surely has a claim against those publications and broadcasts that invade privacy. Certain to come before the Court is the legality of electronic eavesdropping. We mentioned this earlier in regard to police methods and criminal law. But what of electronic listening that is done by one private citizen against another?

"Bugs" placed in telephones or other locations can permit eavesdropping a continent away to learn industrial secrets, travel plans, advertising or sales campaigns, indiscretions which might be used for blackmail or slander, or simply harassment by those who disagree.

Surely laws may be passed and the courts will have to rule on whether a person has a right to privacy, how it may be invaded and what use may be made of information learned in the invasion.

There are a number of other areas not touched upon in this book. Antitrust laws continue to be a big issue before the Court, and the Justices will be asked many times in years to come to rule on whether large companies are restraining trade. Railroad and other business mergers now taking place may well pose judicial questions, as will some ticklish problems growing out of private ownership and government regulation of space satellites. Labor disputes continue to pose problems for the high court.

But for the most part the problems that are discussed in the preceding chapters of this book form the central judicial issues of our times and of the times ahead.

These issues mean a challenging time for the Supreme Court and an exciting time in which to observe the Court. As has been noted, a number of the Justices are elderly. The membership of the Court will change, and with each new member will come new attitudes on these key issues. The balance between liberal and conservative, judicial activism and judicial restraint, states' rights versus federal responsibilities will change—and change many times in the years ahead. The Court's active role in government may well succumb to a period of quiescence in which the *status quo* is embraced. Although it seems unlikely, every one of the precedent-shattering rulings of the last decade could be overruled.

As this book has tried to show, the high court will be most effective as it is successful in embracing dominant opinion, although there can be no doubt that it also plays a powerful role in shaping that opinion. It certainly has shaped public thinking in regard to civil rights, criminal procedures, religious freedom and equal representation. What other changes may be wrought in the future?

Certainly any well-informed person should stay abreast of events inside the Marble Palace, as well as the conflicts and controversies resulting from its decisions.

SUGGESTED READINGS

BICKEL, ALEXANDER M., *The Least Dangerous Branch*. Bobbs-Merrill, Indianapolis, 1962.

CLAYTON, JAMES E., *The Making of Justice*. E. P. Dutton & Co., New York, 1964. A superior, highly readable account of the Supreme Court in action during one historic term.

ERNST, MORRIS L., and Schwartz, Alan U., *Privacy, The Right to Be Let Alone*. The Macmillan Company, New York, 1962.

FRANK, JOHN P., *Marble Palace*. Alfred A. Knopf, New York, 1958. An understandable, if now somewhat dated, account of how the Court operates.

FRANK, JOHN P., *The Warren Court*. The Macmillan Company, New York, 1964. Photographs of the Justices by Yousuf Karsh of Ottawa and biographical sketches of each member.

GARRATY, JOHN A., editor, *Quarrels That Have Shaped the Constitution*. Harper & Row, New York, 1964. Superb. Should be "must" reading.

HYNEMAN, CHARLES S., *The Supreme Court on Trial*. Atherton Press, New York, 1963. Somewhat biased, obtuse, but helpful.

KILPATRICK, JAMES JACKSON, *The Southern Case for School Segregation*. The Crowell-Collier Press, New York, 1962.

LEWIS, ANTHONY, *Gideon's Trumpet*. Random House, New York, 1964. An excellent, highly absorbing account of *Gideon v. Wainwright*.

MARNELL, WILLIAM H., *The First Amendment*. Doubleday & Co., Inc., Garden City, New York, 1964. An excellent account of the quest for religious freedom in America.

MASON, ALPHEUS THOMAS, *The Supreme Court: Palladium of Freedom*. University of Michigan Press, Ann Arbor, 1962. A readable history.

MCCLOSKEY, ROBERT G., *The American Supreme Court*. University of Chicago Press, Chicago, 1960.

MURPHY, WALTER F., *Congress and the Court*. University of Chicago Press, Chicago, 1962. An examination of congressional fury and frustration with the Court.

ROSTOW, EUGENE V., *The Sovereign Prerogative*. Yale University Press, New Haven, 1962.

BROWN V. BOARD OF EDUCATION

OF TOPEKA

347 U.S. 483

1954

WARREN, C. J.: These cases come to us from the States of Kansas, South Carolina, Virginia, and Delaware. They are premised on different facts and different local conditions, but a common legal question justifies their consideration together in this consolidated opinion.

In each of the cases, minors of the Negro race, through their legal representatives, seek the aid of the courts in obtaining admission to the public schools of their community on a nonsegregated basis. In each instance, they have been denied admission to schools attended by white children under laws requiring or permitting segregation according to race. This segregation was alleged to deprive the plaintiffs of the equal protection of the laws under the Fourteenth Amendment. In each of the cases other than the Delaware case, a three-judge federal district court denied relief to the plaintiffs on the so-called "separate but equal" doctrine announced by this Court in Plessy v. Ferguson, 163 U.S. 537. Under that doctrine, equality of treatment is accorded when the races are provided substantially equal facilities, even though these facilities be separate. In the Delaware case, the Supreme Court of Delaware adhered to that doctrine, but ordered that the plaintiffs be admitted to the white schools because of their superiority to the Negro schools.

The plaintiffs contend that segregated public schools are not "equal" and cannot be made "equal," and that hence they are deprived of the equal protection of the laws. Because of the obvious importance of the question presented, the Court took jurisdiction. Argument was heard in the 1952 Term, and reargument was heard this Term on certain questions propounded by the Court.

Reargument was largely devoted to the circumstances surrounding the adoption of the Fourteenth Amendment in 1868. It covered exhaustively consideration of the Amendment in Congress, ratification by the states, then existing practices in racial segregation, and the views of proponents and opponents of the Amendment. This discussion and our own investigation convince us that, although these sources cast some light, it is not enough to resolve the problem with which we are faced. At best, they are inconclusive. The most avid proponents of the post-War Amendments undoubtedly intended them to remove all legal distinctions among "all persons born or naturalized in the United States." Their opponents, just as certainly, were antagonistic to both the letter and the spirit of the Amendments and wished them to have the most limited effect. What others in Congress and the state legislatures had in mind cannot be determined with any degree of certainty.

An additional reason for the inconclusive nature of the Amendment's history, with respect to segregated schools, is the status of public education at that time. In the South, the movement toward free common schools, supported by general taxation, had not yet taken hold. Education of white children was largely in the hands of private groups. Education of Negroes was almost nonexistent, and practically all of the race were illiterate. In fact, any education of Negroes was forbidden by law in some states. Today, in contrast, many Negroes have achieved outstanding success in the arts and sciences as well as in the business and professional world. It is true that public education had already advanced further in the North, but the effect of the Amendment on Northern States was generally ignored in the congressional debates. Even in the North, the conditions of public education did not approximate those existing today. The curriculum was usually rudimentary; ungraded schools were common in rural areas; the school term was but three months a year in many states; and compulsory school attendance was virtually unknown. As a consequence, it is not surprising that there should be so little in the history of the Fourteenth Amendment relating to its intended effect on public education.

In the first cases in this Court construing the Fourteenth Amendment, decided shortly after its adoption, the Court interpreted it as proscribing all state-imposed discriminations against the Negro race. The doctrine of "separate but equal" did not make its appearance in this Court until 1896 in the case of Plessy v. Ferguson, *supra*, involving not education but transportation. American courts have since labored with the doctrine for over half a century. In this Court, there have been six cases involving the "separate but equal" doctrine in the field of public education. In Cumming v. Board of Education of Richmond County, 175 U.S. 528, and Gong Lum v. Rice, 275 U.S. 78, the validity of the doctrine itself was not challenged. In more recent cases, all on the graduate school level, inequality was found in that specific benefits enjoyed by white students were denied to Negro students of the same educational qualifications. State of Missouri *ex rel.* Gaines v. Canada, 305 U.S. 337; Sipuel v. Board of Regents of University of Oklahoma, 332 U. S. 631; Sweatt v. Painter, 339 U.S. 629; McLaurin v. Oklahoma State Regents, 339 U.S. 637. In none of these cases was it necessary to reexamine the doctrine to grant relief to the Negro plaintiff. And in Sweatt v. Painter, *supra,* the Court expressly reserved decision on the question whether Plessy v. Ferguson should be held inapplicable to public education.

In the instant cases, that question is directly presented. Here, unlike Sweatt v. Painter, there are findings below that the Negro and white schools involved have been equalized, or are being equalized, with respect to buildings, curricula, qualifications and salaries of teachers, and other "tangible" factors. Our decision, therefore, cannot turn on merely a comparison of these tangible factors in the Negro and white schools involved in each of the cases. We must look instead to the effect of segregation itself on public education.

In approaching this problem, we cannot turn the clock back to 1868 when the Amendment was adopted, or even to 1896 when Plessy v. Ferguson was written. We must consider public education in the light of its full development and its present place in American life throughout the Nation. Only in this way can it be determined if segregation in public schools deprives these plaintiffs of the equal protection of the laws.

Today, education is perhaps the most important function of state and local governments. Compulsory school-attendance laws and the great expenditures for education both demonstrate our recognition of the importance of education to our democratic society. It is required in the performance of our most basic public responsibilities, even service in the armed forces. It is the very foundation of good citizenship. Today it is a principal instrument in awakening the child to cultural values, in preparing him for later professional training, and in helping him to adjust normally to his environment. In these days, it is doubtful that any child may reasonably be expected to succeed in life if he is denied the opportunity of an education. Such an opportunity, where the state has undertaken to provide it, is a right which must be made available to all on equal terms.

We come then to the question presented: Does segregation of children in public schools solely on the basis of race, even though the physical facilities and other "tangible" factors may be equal, deprive the children of the minority group of equal educational opportunities? We believe that it does.

In Sweatt v. Painter, *supra* (339 U.S. 629, 70 S.Ct. 850), in finding that a segregated law school for Negroes could not provide them equal educational opportunities, this Court relied in large part on "those qualities which are incapable of objective measurement but which make for greatness in a law school." In McLaurin v. Oklahoma State Regents, *supra* (339 U.S. 637, 70 S.Ct. 853), the Court, in requiring that a Negro admitted to a white graduate school be treated like all other students, again resorted to intangible considerations: ". . . his ability to study, to engage in discussions and exchange views with other students, and, in general, to learn his profession." Such considerations apply with added force to children in grade and high schools. To separate them from others of similar age and qualifications solely because of their race generates a feeling of inferiority as to their status in the community that may affect their hearts and minds in a way unlikely ever to be undone. The effect of this separation on their educational opportunities was well stated by a finding in the Kansas case by a court which nevertheless felt compelled to rule against the Negro plaintiffs:

"Segregation of white and colored children in public schools has a detrimental effect upon the colored children. The impact is greater when it has the sanction of the law; for the policy of separating the races is usually interpreted as denoting the inferiority of the Negro group. A sense of inferiority affects the motivation of a child to learn. Segregation with the sanction of law, therefore, has a tendency to retard the educational and mental development of Negro children and to deprive them of some of the benefits they would receive in a racially integrated school system."

Whatever may have been the extent of psychological knowledge at the time of Plessy v. Ferguson, this finding is amply supported by modern authority. Any language in Plessy v. Ferguson contrary to this finding is rejected.

We conclude that in the field of public education the doctrine of "separate but equal" has no place. Separate educational facilities are inherently unequal. Therefore, we hold that the plaintiffs and others similarly situated for whom the actions have been brought are, by reason of the segregation complained of, deprived of the equal protection of the laws guaranteed by the Fourteenth Amendment. This disposition makes unnecessary any discussion whether such segregation also violates the Due-Process Clause of the Fourteenth Amendment.

Because these are class actions, because of the wide applicability of this decision, and because of the great variety of local conditions, the formulation of decrees in these cases presents problems of considerable complexity. On reargument, the consideration of appropriate relief was necessarily subordinated to the primary question—the constitutionality of segregation in public education. We have now announced that such segregation is a denial of the equal protection of the laws. In order that we may have the full assistance of the parties in formulating decrees, the cases will be restored to the docket, and the parties are requested to present further argument. . . . The Attorney General of the United States is again invited to participate. The Attorneys General of the states requiring or permitting segregation in public education will also be permitted to appear as *amici curiae* upon request to do so by September 15, 1954, and submission of briefs by October 1, 1954.

It is so ordered.

THE CONSTITUTION
OF THE UNITED STATES

We the People of the United States, in Order to form a more perfect Union, establish Justice, insure domestic Tranquility, provide for the common defence, promote the general Welfare, and secure the Blessings of Liberty to ourselves and our Posterity, do ordain and establish this Constitution for the United States of America.

ARTICLE I

Section 1. All legislative Powers herein granted shall be vested in a Congress of the United States, which shall consist of a Senate and House of Representatives.

Section 2. The House of Representatives shall be composed of Members chosen every second Year by the People of the several States, and the Electors in each State shall have the Qualifications requisite for Electors of the most numerous Branch of the State Legislature.

No Person shall be a Representative who shall not have attained to the Age of twenty-five Years, and been seven Years a Citizen of the United States, and who shall not, when elected, be an inhabitant of that State in which he shall be chosen.

Representatives and direct Taxes shall be apportioned among the several States which may be included within this Union, according to their respective Numbers, [which shall be determined by adding to the whole Number of free Persons, including those bound to Service for a Term of Years, and excluding Indians not taxed, three-fifths of all other Persons.][1] The actual Enumeration shall be made within three Years after the first Meeting of the Congress of the United States, and within every subsequent Term of ten Years, in such Manner as they shall by law direct. The Number of Representatives shall not exceed one for every thirty Thousand, but each State shall have at Least one Representative; and until such enumeration shall be made, the State of New Hampshire shall be entitled to chuse three, Massachusetts eight, Rhode-Island and Providence

[1] Superseded by the Fourteenth Amendment.

155

Plantations one, Connecticut five, New-York six, New Jersey four, Pennsylvania eight, Delaware one, Maryland six, Virginia ten, North Carolina five, South Carolina five, and Georgia three.

When vacancies happen in the Representation from any State, the Executive Authority thereof shall issue Writs of Election to fill such Vacancies.

The House of Representatives shall chuse their Speaker and other Officers; and shall have the sole Power of Impeachment.

Section 3. The Senate of the United States shall be composed of two Senators from each State, [chosen by the Legislature thereof,][2] for six Years; and each Senator shall have one Vote.

Immediately after they shall be assembled in Consequence of the first Election, they shall be divided as equally as may be into three Classes. The Seats of the Senators of the first Class shall be vacated at the Expiration of the second Year, of the second Class at the Expiration of the fourth Year, and of the third Class at the Expiration of the sixth Year, so that one third may be chosen every second Year; [and if Vacancies happen by Resignation, or otherwise, during the Recess of the Legislature of any State, the Executive thereof may make temporary Appointments until the next Meeting of the Legislature, which shall then fill such Vacancies.][3]

No Person shall be a Senator who shall not have attained to the

[2] Superseded by the Seventeenth Amendment.

[3] Modified by the Seventeenth Amendment.

Age of thirty Years, and been nine Years a Citizen of the United States, and who shall not, when elected, be an Inhabitant of that State for which he shall be chosen.

The Vice President of the United States shall be President of the Senate, but shall have no Vote, unless they be equally divided.

The Senate shall chuse their other Officers, and also a President pro tempore, in the Absence of the Vice President, or when he shall exercise the Office of President of the United States.

The Senate shall have the sole Power to try all Impeachments. When sitting for that Purpose, they shall be on Oath or Affirmation. When the President of the United States is tried, the Chief Justice shall preside: and no Person shall be convicted without the Concurrence of two-thirds of the Members present.

Judgment in Cases of Impeachment shall not extend further than to removal from Office, and disqualification to hold and enjoy any Office of honor, Trust or Profit under the United States: but the Party convicted shall nevertheless be liable and subject to Indictment, Trial, Judgment and Punishment, according to Law.

Section 4. The Times, Places and Manner of holding Elections for Senators and Representatives, shall be prescribed in each State by the Legislature thereof; but the Congress may at any time by Law make or alter such Regulations, except as to the Places of chusing Senators.

[The Congress shall assemble at least once in every Year, and such

Meeting shall be on the first Monday in December, unless they shall by Law appoint a different Day.]⁴

Section 5. Each House shall be the Judge of the Elections, Returns and Qualifications of its own Members, and a Majority of each shall constitute a Quorum to do Business; but a smaller Number may adjourn from day to day, and may be authorized to compel the Attendance of absent Members, in such Manner, and under such Penalties as each House may provide.

Each House may determine the Rules of its Proceedings, punish its Members for disorderly Behaviour, and, with the Concurrence of two-thirds, expel a Member.

Each House shall keep a Journal of its Proceedings, and from time to time publish the same, excepting such Parts as may in their Judgment require Secrecy; and the Yeas and Nays of the Members of either House on any question shall, at the Desire of one-fifth of those Present, be entered on the Journal.

Neither House, during the Session of Congress, shall, without the Consent of the other, adjourn for more than three days, nor to any other Place than that in which the two Houses shall be sitting.

Section 6. The Senators and Representatives shall receive a Compensation for their Services, to be ascertained by Law, and paid out of the Treasury of the United States. They shall in all Cases, except Treason, Felony and Breach of the Peace, be privileged from Arrest during their Attendance at

⁴ Superseded by the Twentieth Amendment.

the Session of their respective Houses, and in going to and returning from the same; and for any Speech or Debate in either House, they shall not be questioned in any other Place.

No Senator or Representative shall, during the Time for which he was elected, be appointed to any civil Office under the Authority of the United States, which shall have been created, or the Emoluments whereof shall have been encreased during such time; and no Person holding any Office under the United States, shall be a Member of either House during his Continuance in Office.

Section 7. All bills for raising Revenue shall originate in the House of Representatives; but the Senate may propose or concur with Amendments as on other Bills.

Every Bill which shall have passed the House of Representatives and the Senate, shall, before it become a Law, be presented to the President of the United States; If he approve he shall sign it, but if not he shall return it, with his Objections to that House in which it shall have originated, who shall enter the Objections at large on their Journal, and proceed to reconsider it. If after such Reconsideration two-thirds of that House shall agree to pass the Bill, it shall be sent, together with the Objections, to the other House, by which it shall likewise be reconsidered, and if approved by two-thirds of that House, it shall become a Law. But in all such Cases the Votes of both Houses shall be determined by yeas and Nays, and the Names of the Persons voting for and against the Bill shall be entered on the Journal of each House respectively. If any Bill shall not be returned by the President within ten Days (Sundays excepted) after it shall have been presented to him, the Same shall be a Law, in like Manner as if he had signed it, unless the Congress by their Adjournment prevent its Return, in which Case it shall not be a Law.

Every Order, Resolution, or Vote to which the Concurrence of the Senate and House of Representatives may be necessary (except on a question of Adjournment) shall be presented to the President of the United States; and before the Same shall take Effect, shall be approved by him, or being disapproved by him, shall be repassed by two thirds of the Senate and House of Representatives, according to the Rules and Limitations prescribed in the Case of a Bill.

Section 8. The Congress shall have Power To lay and collect Taxes, Duties, Imposts and Excises, to pay the Debts and provide for the common Defence and general Welfare of the United States; but all Duties, Imposts and Excises shall be uniform throughout the United States;

To borrow Money on the credit of the United States;

To regulate Commerce with foreign Nations, and among the several States, and with the Indian Tribes;

To establish a uniform Rule of Naturalization, and uniform Laws on the subject of Bankruptcies throughout the United States;

To coin Money, regulate the Value thereof, and of foreign Coin, and fix the Standard of Weights and Measures;

To provide for the Punishment of counterfeiting the Securities and current Coin of the United States;

To establish Post Offices and post Roads;

To promote the Progress of Science and useful Arts, by securing for limited Times to Authors and Inventors the exclusive Right to their respective Writings and Discoveries;

To constitute Tribunals inferior to the supreme Court;

To define and punish Piracies and Felonies committed on the high Seas, and Offences against the Law of Nations;

To declare War, grant Letters of Marque and Reprisal, and make Rules concerning Captures on Land and Water;

To raise and support Armies, but no Appropriation of Money to that Use shall be for a longer Term than two Years;

To provide and maintain a Navy;

To make Rules for the Government and Regulation of the land and naval Forces;

To provide for calling forth the Militia to execute the Laws of the Union, suppress Insurrections and repel Invasions;

To provide for organizing, arming, and disciplining, the Militia, and for governing such Part of them as may be employed in the Service of the United States, reserving to the States respectively, the Appointment of the Officers, and the Authority of training the Military according to the discipline prescribed by Congress;

To exercise exclusive Legislation

in all Cases whatsoever, over such District (not exceeding ten Miles square) as may, by Cession of particular States, and the Acceptance of Congress, become the Seat of the Government of the United States, and to exercise like Authority over all Places purchased by the Consent of the Legislature of the State in which the Same shall be, for the Erection of Forts, Magazines, Arsenals, dock-Yards, and other needful Buildings;—And

To make all Laws which shall be necessary and proper for carrying into Execution the foregoing Powers, and all other Powers vested by this Constitution in the Government of the United States, or in any Department or Officer thereof.

Section 9. The Migration or Importation of such Persons as any of the States now existing shall think proper to admit, shall not be prohibited by the Congress prior to the Year one thousand eight hundred and eight, but a Tax or duty may be imposed on such Importation, not exceeding ten dollars for each Person.

The Privilege of the Writ of Habeas Corpus shall not be suspended, unless when in Cases of Rebellion or Invasion the public safety may require it.

No Bill of Attainder or ex post facto Law shall be passed.

No Capitation, or other direct, Tax shall be laid, unless in Proportion to the Census or Enumeration herein before directed to be taken.[5]

No Tax or Duty shall be laid on Articles exported from any State.

No Preference shall be given by any Regulation of Commerce or

[5] Modified by the Sixteenth Amendment.

Revenue to the Ports of one State over those of another; nor shall Vessels bound to, or from, one State, be obliged to enter, clear, or pay Duties in another.

No money shall be drawn from the Treasury, but in Consequence of Appropriations made by Law; and a regular Statement and Account of the Receipts and Expenditures of all public Money shall be published from time to time.

No Title of Nobility shall be granted by the United States: And no Person holding any Office of Profit or Trust under them, shall, without the Consent of the Congress, accept any present, Emolument, Office, or Title, of any kind whatever, from any King, Prince, or foreign State.

Section 10. No State shall enter into any Treaty, Alliance, or Confederation; grant Letters of Marque and Reprisal; coin Money; emit Bills of Credit; make any Thing but gold and silver Coin a Tender in Payment of Debts; pass any Bill of Attainder, ex post facto Law, or Law impairing the Obligation of Contracts, or grant any Title of Nobility.

No State shall, without the Consent of the Congress, lay any Imposts or Duties on Imports or Exports, except what may be absolutely necessary for executing its inspection laws; and the net Produce of all Duties and Imposts, laid by any State on Imports or Exports, shall be for the Use of the Treasury of the United States; and all such Laws shall be subject to the Revision, and Control of the Congress.

No State shall, without the Consent of Congress, lay any Duty of

Tonnage, keep Troops, or Ships of War in time of Peace, enter into any Agreement or Compact with another State, or with a foreign Power, or engage in War, unless actually invaded, or in such imminent Danger as will not admit of delay.

ARTICLE II

Section 1. The executive Power shall be vested in a President of the United States of America. He shall hold his Office during the Term of four Years, and, together with the Vice President, chosen for the same Term, be elected, as follows.

Each State shall appoint, in such Manner as the Legislature thereof may direct, a Number of Electors, equal to the whole Number of Senators and Representatives to which the State may be entitled in the Congress: but no Senator or Representative, or Person holding an Office of Trust or Profit under the United States, shall be appointed an Elector.

[The Electors shall meet in their respective States, and vote by Ballot for two Persons, of whom one at least shall not be an Inhabitant of the same State with themselves. And they shall make a List of all the Persons voted for, and the Number of Votes for each; which list they shall sign and certify, and transmit sealed to the Seat of the Government of the United States, directed to the President of the Senate. The President of the Senate shall, in the Presence of the Senate and House of Representatives, open all the Certificates, and the Votes shall then be counted. The person having the greatest Number of Votes shall be the President, if such Number be a Majority of the whole Number of Electors appointed; and if there be more than one who have such Majority, and have an equal Number of Votes, then the House of Representatives shall immediately chuse by Ballot one of them for President; and if no Person have a Majority, then from the five highest on the List the said House shall in like Manner chuse the President. But in chusing the President, the Votes shall be taken by States, the Representation from each State having one Vote; A quorum for this purpose shall consist of a Member or Members from two thirds of the States, and a Majority of all the States shall be necessary to a Choice. In every Case, after the Choice of the President, the Person having the greatest Number of Votes of the Electors shall be the Vice President. But if there should remain two or more who have equal Votes, the Senate chuse from them by Ballot the Vice President.][6]

The Congress may determine the Time of chusing the Electors, and the Day on which they shall give their Votes; which Day shall be the same throughout the United States.

No Person except a natural born Citizen, or a Citizen of the United States, at the time of the Adoption of this Constitution, shall be eligible to the Office of President; neither shall any Person be eligible to that Office who shall not have at-

6 Superseded by the Twelfth Amendment.

tained to the Age of thirty-five Years, and been fourteen Years a Resident within the United States.

In Case of the Removal of the President from Office, or of his Death, Resignation, or Inability to discharge the Powers and Duties of the said Office, the Same shall devolve on the Vice President, and the Congress may by Law provide for the Case of Removal, Death, Resignation or Inability, both of the President and Vice President, declaring what Officer shall then act as President, and such Officer shall act accordingly, until the Disability be removed, or a President shall be elected.

The President shall, at stated Times receive for his Services, a Compensation, which shall neither be encreased nor diminished during the Period for which he shall have been elected, and he shall not receive within that Period any other Emolument from the United States, or any of them.

Before he enter on the Execution of his Office, he shall take the following Oath or Affirmation:—"I do solemnly swear (or affirm) that I will faithfully execute the Office of President of the United States, and will to the best of my Ability, preserve, protect and defend the Constitution of the United States."

Section 2. The President shall be Commander in Chief of the Army and Navy of the United States, and of the Militia of the several States, when called into the actual Service of the United States; he may require the Opinion, in writing, of the principal Officer in each of the executive Departments, upon any Subject relating to the Duties of their respective Offices, and he shall have Power to grant Reprieves and Pardons for Offenses against the United States, except in Cases of Impeachment.

He shall have Power, by and with the Advice and Consent of the Senate, to make Treaties, provided two-thirds of the Senators present concur; and he shall nominate, and by and with the Advice and Consent of the Senate, shall appoint Ambassadors, other public Ministers and Consuls, Judges of the supreme Court, and all other Officers of the United States, whose Appointments are not herein otherwise provided for, and which shall be established by Law: but the Congress may by Law vest the Appointment of such inferior Officers, as they think proper, in the President alone, in the Courts of Law, or in the Heads of Departments.

The President shall have Power to fill up all Vacancies that may happen during the Recess of the Senate, by granting Commissions which shall expire at the End of their next Session.

Section 3. He shall from time to time give to the Congress Information of the State of the Union, and recommend to their Consideration such Measures as he shall judge necessary and expedient; he may, on extraordinary Occasions, convene both Houses, or either of them, and in Case of Disagreement between them, with Respect to the Time of Adjournment, he may adjourn them to such Time as he shall think proper; he shall receive Ambassadors and other public

Ministers; he shall take Care that the Laws be faithfully executed, and shall Commission all Officers of the United States.

Section 4. The President, Vice President and all civil Officers of the United States, shall be removed from Office on Impeachment for, and Conviction of, Treason, Bribery, or other high Crimes and Misdemeanors.

ARTICLE III

Section 1. The judicial Powers of the United States, shall be vested in one supreme Court, and in such inferior Courts as the Congress may from time to time ordain and establish. The Judges, both of the supreme and inferior Courts, shall hold their Offices during good Behaviour, and shall, at stated Times, receive for their Services, a Compensation, which shall not be diminished during their Continuance in Office.

Section 2. The judicial Power shall extend to all Cases, in Law and Equity, arising under this Constitution, the Laws of the United States, and Treaties made, or which shall be made, under their Authority;—to all Cases affecting Ambassadors, other public Ministers and Consuls;—to all Cases of admiralty and maritime Jurisdiction;—to Controversies to which the United States shall be a Party;—to Controversies between two or more States;—between a State and Citizens of another State;[7]—between Citizens of different States,—between Citizens of the same State

7 Modified by the Eleventh Amendment.

claiming Lands under Grants of different States, and between a State, or the Citizens thereof, and foreign States, Citizens or Subjects.

In all cases affecting Ambassadors, other public Ministers and Consuls, and those in which a State shall be Party, the supreme Court shall have original Jurisdiction. In all the other Cases before mentioned, the supreme Court shall have appellate Jurisdiction, both as to Law and Fact, with such Exceptions, and under such Regulations as the Congress shall make.

The Trial of all Crimes, except in Cases of Impeachment, shall be by Jury; and such Trial shall be held in the State where the said Crimes shall have been committed; but when not committed within any State, the Trial shall be at such Place or Places as the Congress may by Law have directed.

Section 3. Treason against the United States, shall consist only in levying War against them, or in adhering to their Enemies, giving them Aid and Comfort. No Person shall be convicted of Treason unless on the Testimony of two Witnesses to the same overt Act, or on Confession in open Court.

The Congress shall have Power to declare the Punishment of Treason, but no Attainder of Treason shall work Corruption of Blood, or Forfeiture except during the Life of the Person attainted.

ARTICLE IV

Section 1. Full Faith and Credit shall be given in each State to the public Acts, Records, and judicial Proceedings of every other State. And the Congress may by general Laws prescribe the Manner in which such Acts, Records and Proceedings shall be proved, and the Effect thereof.

Section 2. The Citizens of each State shall be entitled to all Privileges and Immunities of Citizens in the several States.

A Person charged in any State with Treason, Felony, or other Crime, who shall flee from Justice, and be found in another State, shall on Demand of the executive Authority of the State from which he fled, be delivered up, to be removed to the State having Jurisdiction of the Crime.

No Person held to Service or Labour in one State, under the Laws thereof, escaping into another, shall, in Consequence of any Law or Regulation therein, be discharged from such Service or Labour, but shall be delivered up on Claim of the Party to whom such Service or Labour may be due.

Section 3. New States may be admitted by the Congress into this Union; but no new State shall be formed or erected within the Jurisdiction of any other State; nor any State be formed by the Junction of two or more States, or Parts of States, without the Consent of the Legislatures of the States concerned as well as of the Congress.

The Congress shall have Power to dispose of and make all needful Rules and Regulations respecting the Territory or other Property belonging to the United States; and nothing in this Constitution shall be so construed as to Prejudice any Claims of the United States, or of any particular State.

Section 4. The United States shall guarantee to every State in this Union a Republican Form of Government, and shall protect each of them against Invasion; and on Application of the Legislature, or of the Executive (when the Legislature cannot be convened) against domestic Violence.

ARTICLE V

The Congress, whenever two thirds of both Houses shall deem it necessary, shall propose Amendments to this Constitution, or, on the Application of the Legislatures of two thirds of the several States, shall call a Convention for proposing Amendments, which, in either Case, shall be valid to all Intents and Purposes, as Part of this Constitution, when ratified by the Legislatures of three-fourths of the several States, or by Conventions in three-fourths thereof, as the one or the other Mode of Ratification may be proposed by the Congress; Provided that no Amendment which may be made prior to the Year One thousand eight hundred and eight shall in any Manner affect the first and fourth Clauses in the Ninth Section of the first Article; and that no State, without its Consent, shall be deprived of its equal Suffrage in the Senate.

ARTICLE VI

All Debts contracted and Engagements entered into, before the

Adoption of this Constitution, shall be as valid against the United States under this Constitution, as under the Confederation.

This Constitution, and the Laws of the United States which shall be made in Pursuance thereof; and all Treaties made, or which shall be made, under the Authority of the United States, shall be the supreme Law of the Land; and the Judges in every State shall be bound thereby, any Thing in the Constitution or Laws of any State to the Contrary notwithstanding.

The Senators and Representatives before mentioned, and the Members of the several State Legislatures, and all executive and judicial Officers, both of the United States and of the several States, shall be bound by Oath or Affirmation, to support this Constitution; but no religious Test shall ever be required as a Qualification to any Office or public Trust under the United States.

ARTICLE VII

The Ratification of the Conventions of nine States, shall be sufficient for the Establishment of this Constitution between the States so ratifying the Same.

[Signatures omitted.]

[AMENDMENTS]

ARTICLES in addition to, and Amendment of the Constitution of the United States of America, proposed by Congress, and ratified by the Legislatures of the several States, pursuant to the fifth Article of the original Constitution.

[The first ten articles proposed 25 Sept. 1789; declared in force 15 Dec. 1791]

ARTICLE I

Congress shall make no law respecting an establishment of religion, or prohibiting the free exercise thereof; or abridging the freedom of speech, or of the press; or the right of the people peaceably to assemble, and to petition the Government for a redress of grievances.

ARTICLE II

A well regulated Militia, being necessary to the security of a free State, the right of the people to keep and bear Arms, shall not be infringed.

ARTICLE III

No Soldier shall, in time of peace, be quartered in any house, without the consent of the Owner, nor in time of war, but in a manner to be prescribed by law.

ARTICLE IV

The right of the people to be secure in their persons, houses, papers, and effects, against unreasonable searches and seizures, shall not be violated, and no Warrants shall issue, but upon probable cause, supported by Oath or affirmation, and particularly describing the place to be searched, and the persons or things to be seized.

ARTICLE V

No person shall be held to answer for a capital, or otherwise infamous crime, unless on a presentment or indictment of a Grand Jury, except in cases arising in the land or naval forces, or in the Militia, when in actual service in time of War or public danger; nor shall any person be subject for the same offense to be twice put in jeopardy of life or limb; nor shall be compelled in any criminal case to be a witness against himself, nor be deprived of life, liberty, or property, without due process of law; nor shall private property be taken for public use, without just compensation.

ARTICLE VI

In all criminal prosecutions, the accused shall enjoy the right to a speedy and public trial, by an impartial jury of the State and district wherein the crime shall have been committed, which district shall have been previously ascertained by law, and to be informed of the nature and cause of the accusation; to be confronted with the witnesses against him; to have compulsory process for obtaining witnesses in his favor, and to have the Assistance of Counsel for his defense.

ARTICLE VII

In Suits at common law, where the value in controversy shall exceed twenty dollars, the right of trial by jury shall be preserved, and no fact tried by a jury, shall be otherwise reexamined in any Court of the United States, than according to the rules of the common law.

ARTICLE VIII

Excessive bail shall not be required, nor excessive fines imposed, nor cruel and unusual punishments inflicted.

ARTICLE IX

The enumeration in the Constitution, of certain rights, shall not be construed to deny or disparage others retained by the people.

ARTICLE X

The powers not delegated to the United States by the Constitution, nor prohibited by it to the States, are reserved to the States respectively, or to the people.

ARTICLE XI [proposed 5 Mar. 1794; declared ratified 8 Jan. 1798]

The Judicial power of the United States shall not be construed to extend to any suit in law or equity, commenced or prosecuted against one of the United States by Citizens of another State, or by Citizens or Subjects of any Foreign State.

ARTICLE XII [proposed 12 Dec. 1803; declared ratified 25 Sept. 1804]

The Electors shall meet in their respective states, and vote by ballot for President and Vice President, one of whom, at least, shall not be an inhabitant of the same state with themselves; they shall name in their ballots the person voted for as President, and in distinct ballots the person voted for as Vice President, and they shall make distinct lists of all persons voted for as President, and of all persons voted for as Vice President, and of the number of votes for each, which lists they shall sign and certify, and transmit sealed to the seat of the government of the United States, directed to the President of the Senate;—The President of the Senate shall, in the presence of the Senate and House of Representatives, open all certificates and the votes shall then be counted;—The person having the greatest number of votes for President, shall be the President, if such number be a majority of the whole number of Electors appointed; and if no person have such majority, then from the persons having the highest numbers not exceeding three on the list of those voted for as President, the House of Representatives shall choose immediately, by ballot, the President. But in choosing the President, the votes shall be taken by states, the representation from

each state having one vote; a quorum for this purpose shall consist of a member or members from two-thirds of the states, and a majority of all the states shall be necessary to a choice. And if the House of Representatives shall not choose a President whenever the right of choice shall devolve upon them, before the fourth day of March next following, then the Vice President shall act as President, as in the case of the death or other constitutional disability of the President.—The person having the greatest number of votes as Vice President, shall be the Vice President, if such number be a majority of the whole number of Electors appointed, and if no person have a majority, then from the two highest numbers on the list, the Senate shall choose the Vice President; a quorum for the purpose shall consist of two-thirds of the whole number of Senators, and a majority of the whole number shall be necessary to a choice. But no person constitutionally ineligible to the office of President shall be eligible to that of Vice President of the United States.

ARTICLE XIII [proposed 1 Feb. 1865; declared ratified 18 Dec. 1865]

Section 1. Neither slavery nor involuntary servitude, except as a punishment for crime whereof the party shall have been duly convicted, shall exist within the United States, or any place subject to their jurisdiction.

Section 2. Congress shall have power to enforce this article by appropriate legislation.

ARTICLE XIV [proposed 16 June 1866; declared ratified 28 July 1868]

Section 1. All persons born or naturalized in the United States, and subject to the jurisdiction thereof, are citizens of the United States and of the State wherein they reside. No State shall make or enforce any law which shall abridge the privileges or immunities of citizens of the United States; nor shall any State deprive any person of life, liberty, or property, without due process of law; nor deny to any person within its jurisdiction the equal protection of the laws.

Section 2. Representatives shall be apportioned among the several States according to their respective numbers, counting the whole number of persons in each State, excluding Indians not taxed. But when the right to vote at any election for the choice of electors for President and Vice President of the United States, Representatives in Congress, the Executive and Judicial officers of a State, or the members of the Legislature thereof, is denied to any of the male inhabitants of such State, being twenty-one years of age, and citizens of the United States, or in any way abridged, except for participation in rebellion, or other crime, the basis of representation therein shall be reduced in the proportion which the number of such male citizens shall bear to the whole number of male citizens twenty-one years of age in such State.

Section 3. No person shall be a Senator or Representative in Congress, or elector of President and Vice President, or hold any office, civil or military, under the United States, or under any State, who, having previously taken an oath, as a member of Congress, or as an officer of the United States, or as a member of any State legislature, or as an executive or judicial officer of any State, to support the Constitution of the United States, shall have engaged in insurrection or rebellion against the same, or given aid and comfort to the enemies thereof. But Congress may by a vote of two-thirds of each House, remove such disability.

Section 4. The validity of the public debt of the United States, authorized by law, including debts incurred for payment of pensions and bounties for services in suppressing insurrection or rebellion, shall not be questioned. But neither the United States nor any state shall assume or pay any debt or obligation incurred in aid of insurrection or rebellion against the United States, or any claim for the loss or emancipation of any slave; but all such debts, obligations, and claims shall be held illegal and void.

Section 5. The Congress shall have power to enforce, by appropriate legislation, the provisions of this article.

ARTICLE XV [proposed 27 Feb. 1869; declared ratified 30 Mar. 1870]

Section 1. The right of citizens of the United States to vote shall not be denied or abridged by the United States or by any State on account of race, color, or previous condition of servitude.

Section 2. The Congress shall have power to enforce this article by appropriate legislation.

ARTICLE XVI [proposed 12 July 1909; declared ratified 25 Feb. 1913]

The Congress shall have power to lay and collect taxes on incomes, from whatever source derived, without apportionment among the several States, and without regard to any census or enumeration.

ARTICLE XVII [proposed 16 May 1912; declared ratified 31 May 1913]

The Senate of the United States shall be composed of two Senators from each State, elected by the people thereof, for six years; and each Senator shall have one vote. The electors in each State shall have the qualifications requisite for electors of the most numerous branch of the State legislatures.

When vacancies happen in the representation of any State in the Senate, the executive authority of such State shall issue writs of election to fill such vacancies: *Provided*, That the legislature of any State may empower the executive thereof to make temporary appointments until the people fill the vacancies by election as the legislature may direct.

This amendment shall not be so construed as to affect the election or term of any Senator chosen before it becomes valid as part of the Constitution.

ARTICLE XVIII [proposed 18 Dec. 1917; declared ratified 29 Jan. 1919; repealed by the 21st Amendment]

Section 1. After one year from the ratification of this article the manufacture, sale, or transportation of intoxicating liquors within, the importation thereof into, or the exportation thereof from the United States and all territory subject to the jurisdiction thereof for beverage purposes is hereby prohibited.

Section 2. The Congress and the several States shall have concurrent power to enforce this article by appropriate legislation.

Section 3. This article shall be inoperative unless it shall have been ratified as an amendment to the Constitution by the legislatures of the several States, as provided in the Constitution, within seven years from the date of the submission hereof to the States by the Congress.[8]

ARTICLE XIX [proposed 4 June 1919; declared ratified 26 Aug. 1920]

[8] Superseded by the Twenty-first Amendment.

The right of citizens of the United States to vote shall not be denied or abridged by the United States or by any State on account of sex.

Congress shall have power to enforce this article by appropriate legislation.

ARTICLE XX [proposed 2 Mar. 1932; declared ratified 6 Feb. 1933]

Section 1. The terms of the President and Vice President shall end at noon on the 20th day of January, and the terms of Senators and Representatives at noon on the 3d day of January, of the years in which such terms would have ended if this article had not been ratified; and the terms of their successors shall then begin.

Section 2. The Congress shall assemble at least once in every year, and such meeting shall begin at noon on the 3d day of January, unless they shall by law appoint a different day.

Section 3. If, at the time fixed for the beginning of the term of the President, the President elect shall have died, the Vice President elect shall become President. If a President shall not have been chosen before the time fixed for the beginning of his term, or if the President elect shall have failed to qualify, then the Vice President elect shall act as President until a President shall have qualified; and the Congress may by law provide for the case wherein neither a President elect nor a Vice President elect shall have qualified, declaring who shall then act as President, or the manner in which one who is to act shall be selected, and such person shall act accordingly until a President or Vice President shall have qualified.

Section 4. The Congress may by law provide for the case of the death of any of the persons from whom the House of Representatives may choose a President whenever the right of choice shall have devolved upon them, and for the case of the death of any of the persons from whom the Senate may choose a Vice President whenever the right of choice shall have devolved upon them.

Section 5. Sections 1 and 2 shall take effect on the 15th day of October following the ratification of this article.

Section 6. This article shall be inoperative unless it shall have been ratified as an amendment to the Constitution by the legislatures of three-fourths of the several States within seven years from the date of its submission.

ARTICLE XXI [proposed 20 Feb. 1933; declared ratified 5 Dec. 1933]

Section 1. The Eighteenth article of amendment to the Constitution of the United States is hereby repealed.

Section 2. The transportation or importation into any State, Territory, or possession of the United States for delivery or use therein of intoxicating liquors, in violation of the laws thereof, is hereby prohibited.

Section 3. This article shall be inoperative unless it shall have been ratified as an amendment to the Constitution by conventions in the several States, as provided in the Constitution, within seven years from the date of the submission hereof to the States by the Congress.

ARTICLE XXII [proposed 24 Mar. 1947; declared ratified 26 Feb. 1951]

Section 1. No person shall be elected to the office of the President more than twice, and no person who has held the office of President, or acted as President, for more than two years of a term to which some other person was elected President shall be elected to the office of the President more than once. But this Article shall not apply to any person holding the office of President when this Article was proposed by the Congress, and shall not prevent any person who may be holding the office of President, or acting as President, during the term within which this Article becomes operative from holding the office of President or acting as President during the remainder of such term.

Section 2. This article shall be inoperative unless it shall have been ratified as an amendment to the Constitution by the legislatures of three-fourths of the several States within seven years from the date of its submission to the States by the Congress.

ARTICLE XXIII [proposed 16 June 1960; declared ratified 3 Apr. 1961]

Section 1. The District constituting the seat of Government of the United States shall appoint in such manner as the Congress may direct: A number of electors of President and Vice President equal to the whole number of Senators and Representatives in Congress to which the District would be entitled if it were a State, but in no event more than the least populous State; they shall be in addition to those appointed by the States, but they shall be considered, for the purposes of the election of President and Vice President, to be electors appointed by a State; and they shall meet in the district and perform such duties as provided by the twelfth article of amendment.

Section 2. The Congress shall have power to enforce this article by appropriate legislation.

ARTICLE XXIV [proposed 27 Aug. 1962; declared ratified 4 Feb. 1964]

Section 1. The right of citizens of the United States to vote in any primary or other election for President or Vice President, for electors for President or Vice President, or for Senator or Representative in Congress, shall not be denied or abridged by the United States or any State by reason of failure to pay any poll tax or other tax.

Section 2. The Congress shall

have power to enforce this article by appropriate legislation.

ARTICLE XXV [proposed 6 July 1965]

Section 1. In case of the removal of the President from office or his death or resignation, the Vice President shall become President.

Section 2. Whenever there is a vacancy in the office of the Vice President, the President shall nominate the Vice President who shall take the office upon confirmation by a majority vote of both houses of Congress.

Section 3. Whenever the President transmits to the President pro tempore of the Senate and the Speaker of the House of Representatives his written declaration that he is unable to discharge the powers and duties of his office, and until he transmits to them a written declaration to the contrary, such powers and duties shall be discharged by the Vice President as Acting President.

Section 4. Whenever the Vice President and a majority of either the principal officers of the executive departments or of such other body as Congress may by law provide, transmit to the President pro tempore of the Senate and the Speaker of the House of Representatives their written declaration that the President is unable to discharge the powers and duties of his office, the Vice President shall immediately assume the powers and duties of the office as Acting President.

Thereafter, when the President transmits to the President pro tempore of the Senate and the Speaker of the House of Representatives his written declaration that no inability exists, he shall resume the powers and duties of his office unless the Vice President and a majority of either the principal officers of the executive department or of such other body as Congress may by law provide, transmit within four days to the President pro tempore of the Senate and the Speaker of the House of Representatives their written declaration that the President is unable to discharge the powers and duties of his office. Thereupon Congress shall decide the issue, assembling within 48 hours for that purpose if not in session. If the Congress, within 21 days after receipt of the latter written declaration, or, if Congress is not in session, within 21 days after Congress is required to assemble, determines by two-thirds vote of both houses that the President is unable to discharge the powers and duties of his office, the Vice President shall continue to discharge the same as Acting President; otherwise, the President shall resume the powers and duties of his office.

INDEX

ROBERT A. LISTON grew up in Ohio and was graduated from Hiram College. Following several years as a journalist, he became a free-lance magazine writer with articles appearing in *Life, The Saturday Evening Post* and *Reader's Digest*. A lifelong interest in the law led to the writing of *Tides of Justice*.

Mr. Liston lives with his wife and three children in Westport, Connecticut, and when not at his work he enjoys swimming and ice skating.